F
o
T
o

Yo

King Arthur's Death

The Alliterative Morte Arthure

Also by Michael Smith
Sir Gawain and the Green Knight (trans.)

King Arthur's Death

The Alliterative Morte Arthure

Translated and Illustrated
by Michael Smith

unbound

This edition first published in 2021

Unbound
TC Group, Level 1, Devonshire House,
One Mayfair Place, London W1J 8AJ

www.unbound.com

Text Design by PDQ

A CIP record for this book is available from the British Library

ISBN 978-1–78352–908-7 (trade hbk)
ISBN 978-1–78352–909-4 (ebook)

Printed and bound by CPI Group (UK) Ltd, Croydon, CR0 4YY

1 3 5 7 9 8 6 4 2

For Adrian

CONTENTS

Dedicated to the memories of my great uncles:

M. T. Knowles; South Lancashire Regiment, d. 28th October 1918
and
E. H. Knowles; Royal Field Artillery, d. 9th November 1918,

two fair sons of Warrington
who fought and fell in France.

Let me speak proudly: tell the constable
We are but warriors for the working-day
Henry V

HISTORICAL INTRODUCTION

King Arthur's Death or *Arthur's Death*, otherwise known as the *Alliterative Morte Arthure*, is acknowledged as one of the jewels to emerge from the fourteenth-century revival in alliterative poetry, a poetic form stretching back at least to Anglo-Saxon times. The quality of the poem is widely seen as being second only to the works of the *Gawain* poet, also known as the *Pearl* poet. Like *Sir Gawain and the Green Knight*, it is a product of provincial England, thought to have been written in the dialect of southern Lincolnshire. While not as sophisticated in style or technique as *Gawain*, nor indeed in the layering of its messages, *King Arthur's Death* is nonetheless an outstanding exemplar of the alliterative technique and is masterful in its use of a newly liberated English language, blossoming during the reigns of Edward III, Richard II and Henry IV. It was also a major source for the Roman Wars section of Sir Thomas Malory's more famous *Le Morte d'Arthur*, which was published by William Caxton in 1485.

The only surviving manuscript of this version of the story is in the 'Lincoln Thornton' manuscript in the library of Lincoln Cathedral (Lincoln MS 91). It was transcribed *c.*1440 by Robert Thornton of East Newton, near York, from an earlier script (or scripts) long since vanished. *King Arthur's Death* is among more than sixteen major works that Thornton transcribed during his lifetime, which include the only complete text of *The Parlement of the Thre Ages* and the tantalisingly incomplete *Wynnere and Wastoure*. These last two appear in a separate, smaller collection of Thornton's work held in the British Library, known as the 'London Thornton' manuscript.

Like many poems of its time, *King Arthur's Death* gained its current title in more recent centuries; it is unclear how the manuscript was originally known. Similarly, despite a line added much later to it at the end ascribing it to Robert Thornton, its actual composer is unknown. However, given its style and highly graphic nature, the poet is assumed to be a man; so throughout, I will refer to the poet as 'he'. While being a key poem of the Alliterative Revival, it also forms a significant component of the Arthurian canon in general, drawing much of its plot and structure from the writings of Geoffrey of Monmouth, Wace, Laȝamon and others (see below). It is the combination of its subject, and its place in the Revival, which make it of particular interest to historians: why was it written at this time and what was its purpose? Elements of the poem help point to a very narrow window of time in which it could have been composed, which may help to answer these questions.

Although the poem has all the qualities of a heroic epic, *King Arthur's Death* is far from being a remote, romantic work and instead pays remarkable attention to contemporary detail in terms of politics, warfare, military organisation and geography. It also exhibits an astonishing insight into human psychology as well as a nuanced approach to the chivalric ideal, contrasting the aesthetic ambitions of chivalry with the harsh realities of war and, indeed, the demands of religious duty. Consequently, the work is not so much an Arthurian romance (the magical experiences of individual knights), nor even a typical mediaeval *chanson de geste* (a song of deeds), but more a cutting observation of the duties of kings in their conduct of war and politics. The message appears to be that power without legitimacy is ultimately flawed, despite the best efforts of those who serve their master. The poem has contemporary relevance.

The Arthurian canon and the poet's sources

Whether or not King Arthur was a real historical figure, his story has its most remote roots in the time after the Romans left Britain early in the fifth century. The seventh-century *Y Gododdin*, by the Welsh poet Aneirin, alludes to him in what is thought to be the first historical mention in literature. The later *Llyfr Du Caerfyrddin* (the *Black Book of Carmarthen*) refers to Arthur as an exalted prisoner. However, the king's character and putative history become more established in the ninth-century *Historia Britonnum*, commonly attributed to the monk Nennius, when Arthur is called *dux bellorum* (a war lord). His story also develops in the tenth-century *Annales Cambriae* (the *Annals of Wales*). Crucially, not one of these works survives in its original form. The extant manuscripts for *Y Gododdin* and the *Llyfr Du* are thought to date from the thirteenth century; Nennius' work, alongside the earliest known copy of the *Annales*, survives in the British Library in a manuscript (Harley, MS 3859) thought to be no earlier in date than the twelfth century.

It is when Geoffrey of Monmouth (c.1095–1155) created his *Historia Regum Britanniae*, the *History of the Kings of Britain* of c.1136, a magnificent – if fantastic – unifying story of Britain, that Arthur became established as a significant historical and literary figure. His work was to spawn a rich canon of Arthurian chronicles and romances which was to stretch over many centuries, including two, by the poets Robert Wace (the *Roman de Brut* c.1155) and Laȝamon (*Laȝamon's Brut* c.1190) which were hugely influential. Wace, embellishing Geoffrey's work, introduces us to the Round Table for the first time; Laȝamon to Arthur's dream of his own downfall (albeit a dream which involves Mordred himself rather than Lady Fortune, as in our poem). Both Wace and Laȝamon were to have a significant impact on later works in the canon; it is in the works of Chrétien de Troyes in France (writing somewhere between 1159 and 1191) that the Arthurian stories begin to blossom. Chrétien's adulterous *Lancelot* and Grail-focused *Perceval* were to help transform the genre, culminating in Malory's great *Le Morte D'Arthur*, whose influence stretches to the present day.

King Arthur's Death forms a key, and intriguing, part of this great corpus of work and draws upon much of it for its plot. However, the focus of the poem is less about the Round Table and chivalric romance and more about warfare and consequence. Hence, while characters such as Sir Lancelot, Sir Kay and Sir Bedevere feature within the narrative, they do so as relatively minor figures. Instead, in its pursuit of a military narrative, the poem chooses to focus on Arthur himself, Sir Cador, Sir Gawain and, of course, Sir Mordred. This reflects the historical division of the Arthur narrative into two main traditions: the romantic (e.g Chrétien de Troyes) and the chronicle (in particular works based on Geoffrey of Monmouth, known as the Galfridian tradition).

Maureen Fries, writing in Göller's *The Alliterative Morte Arthure* (see Further Reading), reveals that while *King Arthur's Death* is strongly placed in the Galfridian tradition it nonetheless draws on elements from romance versions of the story. The poem retains the rage of Arthur from *Laȝamon's Brut* and elements of the Lady Fortune dream from the thirteenth-century French *Mort Artu*; its references to the Nine Worthies (lines 3267–3337 and 3406–3437) are probably drawn from the French *Voeux de Paon* (the Vows of the Peacock) of c.1310. Elsewhere, the Gawain–Priamus episode (2513 onwards) is thought to have derived from the twelfth-century French romance *Fierabras*, while the broader section in which this episode occurs is from another French romance, *Li Fuerres de Gadres*. Crucially, the poem also carries many unique elements of its own, including Mordred's refusal to act as Arthur's regent and Guinevere later bearing Mordred's children. These elements may have been introduced specifically by the poet to further exaggerate Arthur's own folly or to highlight poor decisions and negative consequences which wise kings should seek to avoid.

It is the combination of the chronicle approach with touches of romance which make the poem a fascinating example of the type. Yet it is the poem's detail, brutality and pace, combined with its rich poetic quality and latent political and psychological messages, which transform *King Arthur's Death* from some tedious martial epic into something much grander, and fundamentally deeper. By embellishing the work with a magnificent attention to contemporary detail, the poet also makes it stand out from others of its genre; it is as if he truly is making a point about the society and times in which he lived.

Credibility through detail

Key to the poem's credibility – and its ability to deliver its message without moralising or lecturing its audience – is its inherent realism. *King Arthur's Death* is a masculine work: an epic sweep of battles and conflict, of passion and revenge, of Christianity versus paganism. Despite its allusions to chivalry and the chivalric ideal, this is not a King Arthur tale of knights errant, queens and courtiers, damsels in distress. Indeed, where women feature, they are shown less to highlight the intricacies of chivalric honour and more to illustrate how war debases morality. It is a significant feature of this work that, with the exceptions of the battle with the Giant of Mont Saint Michel and spiritual interludes, such as the appearance of Sir Priamus (perhaps the only two episodes in the work which could be described as a romance), nearly all of its action could be real. Hence, instead of magical lands, the poem places Arthur in real time and space: Carlisle, Sandwich, the Cotentin peninsula, crossing the Alps. When battles are fought, their tactics are reminders of real conflicts: the organisation of armies at Crécy (1346); the horrors of siege warfare at Limoges (1370); the chaining together of ships at the naval battle off Sluys (1340). When the poet describes knights, the heraldry is accurate (for example, when Mordred changes his coat of arms so he cannot be recognised [lines 4181–5]).

The precise attention to detail and the graphic descriptions of battle all seem to point to the fact that the *Arthur*-poet had either been to war, was well read about its impact or was well connected. He has a complex knowledge of arms and armour, referencing types of armour from different periods (e.g. the hauberk) and different countries (the jazerant). Some of his references (e.g. the fewter, a rest for a lance) may aid in dating the work to the early fifteenth century. Yet it is his battle descriptions which place the poem right at the action in the mind of the audience. He describes majestically the shock of troops when they suddenly charge after an initial advance (line 1759) or when they shudder under the impact of an arrow storm (2105–6). He talks about the 'bowmen of Britain' (2095), alluding to their great triumphs at Crécy (August 1346), Poitiers (September 1356) and elsewhere, and describes in detail the devastating effects of the impact of an arrow storm on animals (2099–2100). Intriguingly, he understands the tactical deployment of archers on the battlefield and their supporting troops (1990–92), the knowledge of which is highly specific and still a subject of debate by military historians. His visceral portrayal of entrails being trodden into the ground by horses (2781–3) or of bodies being cut in two by great blades (1388–9) is great theatre but is not a flourish of invention; nor is his evocation of faces disfigured by horses galloping over them (2149–50). Although his descriptions are occasionally repugnant and sometimes exhibit an almost comic black humour, his writing appears almost as a form of reportage: a collation of information gleaned from a wide variety of sources.

The context of the poem

Yet, if detail grounds the poem in reality, what reality are we being asked to consider? What is the historical context? Research suggests that *King Arthur's Death* was written in the final quarter of the fourteenth century or the first decade of the fifteenth century (see below). These years marked a period of political uncertainty in England following the early death in 1376 of Edward, the Black Prince, and the decline of his father, Edward III, who died the following year. Edward had been a warlike and successful king, winning great victories in France; the Black Prince, his eldest son, was an exemplar of the chivalric ideal and a famous, martial knight in the mould of his father. Edward's death resulted in Richard II, the son of the Black Prince, ascending to the throne at the age of ten. This placed the kingdom in the hands of regency councils, heavily influenced by the child-king's uncles, John of Gaunt and Thomas of Woodstock. It wouldn't be until 1389 that Richard would announce his intention to rule as a monarch of full age.

Compared to his ancestors, Richard would be regarded unfavourably as a king, more interested in culture than in pursuing hereditary claims in France. Ascending to the crown at such an early age placed him at a disadvantage; his reign was marked by a reliance on favourites, causing discontent among the English aristocracy. In 1387 a group known as the Lords Appellant took temporary control of the running of the kingdom and, although harmony was restored in the years following 1389, Richard took his revenge in 1397 in a period known as the 'tyranny' when many of the Appellants were executed or banished. It was during this period that Gaunt's son, Henry Bolingbroke, was exiled along with the Duke of Norfolk following an accusation of treason; when Gaunt died in 1399, Henry was disinherited by Richard. However, while Richard was absent in Ireland, Henry returned to England and garnered sufficient support to challenge the king and, indeed, to usurp the crown. Richard himself ended his days at Pontefract Castle in Yorkshire, where he was starved to death in February 1400. It is the instability of Richard's reign, and Henry's subsequent coronation (as Henry IV) in October 1399, which appear to form the backdrop to this magnificent poem. *King Arthur's Death*, in its portrayal of the vulnerability of monarchical authority, is a fabulous mirror on those uncertain years, when Henry IV was determined not only to maintain control but also, crucially, to assert his own royal legitimacy.

The international backdrop is also important. This was the period of the Papal Schism (1378–1417) when dissension and disagreement within the church, following the election of Urban VI in Rome, led to a rival pope, Clement VII, being elected and an alternative papacy being re-established at Avignon, where it had resided for most of the fourteenth century. The Schism led to a ruler siding with one pope in pursuit of his own claims; England in this period supported Urban while France, for example, supported Clement. Hence, the international flavour taken on by Arthur's ventures across Europe to Rome had a distinct contemporary relevance. By adapting Geoffrey of Monmouth's imperial Roman setting of the Arthurian story to European events involving Rome in the fourteenth and early fifteenth centuries, the poet cleverly places the story in a context both real and relevant to its intended audience.

Equally relevant is the figure of the Holy Roman Emperor, a ruler elected by the princes of Germany and crowned by the pope himself; a man who played a key role in the defence of the Catholic faith. The Holy Roman Empire was seen as the successor to the ancient Roman Empire and, in this period, was comprised largely of German and north Italian states. At the time of the writing of *King Arthur's Death*, the notional emperor was Wenceslas IV (1378–1400) followed by Rupert of the Palatinate (1400–10), although neither had been officially crowned by the pope and both were known instead as 'King of the Germans'. Nonetheless, the imperial rule covering Germany, Italy, Bohemia, Hungary and Croatia helps us understand the reference to the '*The emperour of Almayne, and alle theis este marches*' (line 3210). Thus, when Arthur dreams of Lady Fortune presenting him with the regalia befitting of such an emperor (lines 3350–57), a contemporary audience would have understood that in the dream Arthur has reached the very apogee of his powers: leading ruler of all Western Europe. Perhaps, too, he had over-reached himself – and become a victim of his own pride. Being crowned by the pope (who is within his grasp at Rome), Arthur is shown as being a legitimate Holy Roman Emperor and a king above all others. Such an honour was not beyond the bounds of possibility; Edward III was offered the crown in 1348, as was Richard II in 1397.

The honour of such an elevation carried with it a key role in the defending of the Roman Catholic faith. In the poem Lucius, the fictional Emperor of Rome, draws together not only an army of Germans but also expands this dramatically by engaging the support of 'pagans' from Arab lands and beyond. The poet therefore seems to be asking his readers to accept that Lucius, the incumbent (Holy) Roman Emperor, is a danger both to the pope and to Western Europe. Although this is a feature of other poems in the Galfridian tradition, to a contemporary audience this may have had a particular relevance: in 1396 a crusading army assembled to defend Western Europe from Turkish encroachment was defeated by the Ottomans at Nicopolis. A Holy Roman Emperor in league with such forces would have been a threat to the entire Western order; Arthur's role, therefore, is elevated to one of enormous significance. Lucius' engagement with the Ottomans may be seen as a reference to the vulnerability of the European monarchical order. In pointing once more to the need for strong Christian leadership, the poet appears to be positioning his Arthur as more akin to Henry IV, himself a crusading knight who fought in Lithuania and also undertook a pilgrimage to Jerusalem, rather than as a cultural aesthete such as Richard II. In asking his audience to consider the duty of kings to defend the Catholic faith, the poet may also be reflecting on the development of heretical forms of religion in the fourteenth century, such as the rise of the Hussites under Wenceslas and, in particular, the sympathy afforded to the views of John Wyclif and his 'Lollard' followers in England under both John of Gaunt and Richard II (see below).

Message and themes

In an environment of questionable monarchical legitimacy, a Catholic Church split between two competing factors, the growth of perceived heretical views and the rise in power of the Ottomans, a contemporary audience might – like today – be seeking certainty. Many poems of the Alliterative Revival were allegorical or reflective in nature; some, such as the incomplete *Mum and the Sothsegger*, were also satirical and even critical. In penning *King Arthur's Death*, it may well have been the poet's intention to warn against the dangers of foreign wars when the political landscape at home was so unstable. Yet, in a time of distrust and suspicion, he may also have sought to conceal open criticism of the king by dressing the story up as an apparently tame Arthurian chronicle. If so, the poet's use of Geoffrey of Monmouth as a framework for his critique seems both intelligent and inspired; he could craft his message within the uncontroversial structure of a pre-existing and well-known chronicle. In such a setting, the depravity of war is laid out for all to see; the failings of kings laid bare. *King Arthur's Death* lets its readers look behind the stuff and spin of the glories of war and national grandeur to greater horrors: the suffering of all for the dreams of the few.

With careful reading, *King Arthur's Death* can be seen to reflect the political environment of its time, again dressed in the clothes of Arthur. While not an allegorical work per se, if it was written at the end of the fourteenth century, the general approach then appears supportive of a vulnerable Henry Bolingbroke following his usurpation of the crown; he seems to imply that good monarchy is essential to deliver stability. In this light, it has been suggested that Mordred might represent a fallen Richard and that Arthur represents Henry; both characters highlight traits that a just and honest king must seek to avoid if he is to rule well. Mordred shows what happens when a king steals power by treachery; Arthur what can happen to a king if, being victorious, he falls victim to pride, vanity and the pursuit of tyranny. By highlighting the folly of overweening pride – what poets of the Revival called 'surquedry' (e.g. line 2616) – this poem acts as a reference work for good kingship. In lifting Arthur to the heights of Holy Roman Emperor only to toss him down from the Wheel of Fortune, the poet reveals to any king obsessed by power that he is only there by the will of God and that God, in His own caprice, can just as quickly snatch it back.

Yet if the poem appears to advocate firm leadership and a devotion to what is right, it also questions the morality of the way in which leaders gain their power. Throughout there is an astonishing tripartite conflict between competing forces: chivalry, warfare and religion. In *Sir Gawain and the Green Knight*, these themes are addressed in a highly nuanced way, yet here we are shown this trinity in a much more graphic fashion, illustrated again and again as knights in chivalric panoply slay their enemies in the most brutal fashion, and yet at their own end seek confession. This is not in itself unusual; in a society tied to the Christian Church and bound to defend it, its denizens created their own moral codes based firmly around Church and State. This is exemplified in Geoffroi de Charny's *Book of Chivalry* written around 1350.

De Charny's writings – indeed his very actions – are seen as archetypal in the practice of chivalry and the pursuit of honourable war; *King Arthur's Death* often reflects his influence. For example, Arthur is honourable in his treatment of women both in his tearful concern for the Duchess of Brittany following her capture by the Giant of Mont Saint Michel (lines 870–75), and in his gracious actions towards the Duchess of Metz (3057–9). Elsewhere, a knight's duty to his lord is shown by Sir Idrus not leaving Arthur's side to help his own father in distress (4135–54), while the lengthy passage covering Sir Gawain's combat with Sir Priamus (followed by the latter's surrender) might be seem as the spiritual apogee of the chivalric ideal of honour in warfare. Unchivalrous acts are criticised by the poet too; for example, when Sir Kay is struck by his enemy from behind (2171–84), or when Mordred changes his coat of arms to avoid being recognised (4181–5). The poet also seems to lament the unchivalrous nature of modern war when he alludes to the devastation wrought by the longbow: 'Such warfare is foul that so hurts the flesh', he exclaims (2099).

Yet chivalry in *King Arthur's Death* is also deliberately contrasted with reality. It is a curious feature of this poem that while it extols the chivalric ideal through knightly prowess, it nevertheless does not pull any punches concerning the impact of war. When knights are slain, they don't just suffer a generic mortal wound but are wounded specifically and in gory detail. For example, when Sir Florent slays Sir Feraunt (lines 2768–71), the latter's face is disfigured and his brain pierced by the lance. In lines 2167–8, Sir Kay inflicts such damage with his lance that the lungs and the liver of his opponent hang from the shaft. Sir Kay himself is slain by a lance piercing his bowels on line 2175 while Sir Gawain, slicing with his sword, Galuth, reveals the liver of Sir Priamus on line 2561. At times, the poet exhibits a truly dark sense of humour in his descriptions, a feature which decorates the work throughout, for example in lines 2207–9 when King Arthur slices an opponent in half, leaving the man's horse to ride around with the top half of its rider missing; the poet writes 'My hope, true to say, is his wound never heals!'

It has been argued that this presents a realist flavour and that the explicit details would have been seen by its audience as commonplace, in the manner of a literary setting. Certainly, it is difficult for us today to imagine a mediaeval battlefield where combatants by and large were left to die of their wounds, but this was the reality. In such a world, it is easy to understand why deep religious faith is a necessary corollary to violence; both the poet and his characters remind us throughout of their deep beliefs. Arthur's shield carries the Virgin and Child (lines 3648–50); Sir Kay takes confession and kneels in prayer at his death (2195–6); Arthur himself seeks confession of his sins at the end (4314–15); and Sir Priamus seeks conversion to Christianity 2585–8).

Yet the poem appears conflicted in its presentation of chivalric display, brutal killing and religious virtue. How can it be that the slaying of fifty knights (lines 1809–12) is a 'noble' act? How can it be that knights bedecked in jewels and bright colours can cause such slaughter? While the Round Table might be imagined as a group of chivalrous companions, its grounding in war is never far away (2910–13):

> They hew through the helmets   of haughty nobles
> Such that their hilted swords   run down to their hearts,
> And then those renowned ranks   of the Round Table
> Rush down and rive through   those renegade wretches.

The poet's use of contrast between chivalry and bloodshed is fascinating and intriguing. In juxtaposing glamour and panoply with bloodshed and gore, he appears to be working on two levels. Laura Ashe has written that Richard's reign was characterised by a weariness of war and its cost, adding 'more insidious was the sense that the chivalric ideal might itself be empty'. Hence, there is a possibility that the poet is also intending to share an anti-war agenda.

The concept of the 'Just War', a war fought for legitimate aims and sanctioned by the Church, was a significant component of international politics in the mediaeval period (indeed, war today still demands legitimacy if it is to be sanctioned). A key exponent of this at the time of the poem was John Wyclif (c.1330–84), a leading theologian whose followers – a group known as the 'Lollards' – had been protected by both John of Gaunt and Richard II. Reflecting the burgeoning of the English language in the fourteenth century, Wyclif was also a leading force in translating the Bible into English and garnered sufficient support from court and parliament to continue his work, despite its being seen as a threat within the Church as a whole. Significantly, across much of his work, Wyclif also questioned the legitimacy of war and whether it could ever be right to kill another. In this light, is it possible the poet was Wycliffite in his sympathies and was pursuing an additional agenda?

While not graphically in evidence as a theme, it is possible to interpret the poem in this way. Dr Rory Cox (*John Wyclif on War and Peace*) writes, 'The mediaeval just war was understood to operate on a level of interdependency between the three major conditions of just cause, proper authority and correct intention. If any of these conditions was not fulfilled, the entire enterprise was rendered unjust.' Arthur, in facing unjust demands from Lucius at the beginning of the poem, is aggrieved and vengeful, yet he seeks the advice of the Round Table and others (including theologians) before committing to war. In this light, we can see that Arthur is revealing to his audience that he has 'just cause' to go to war with Lucius. The major questions arise, however, concerning whether he has 'proper authority' and, indeed, the 'correct intention'. Certainly, it would seem that, without obtaining the support of the pope, Arthur does not have the proper authority. Indeed, in taking on Lucius – the notional Holy Roman Emperor and king above kings – he is actually challenging the authority of the Holy Church itself. Hence, the poet may also be suggesting that Arthur's intention is not correct; in Just War theory, Arthur has only met one of the three criteria. While Arthur's rage at Lucius for stealing his own lands, and his intention is to reclaim what is rightfully his (his ancestral realms on the continent) might appear legitimate, it is what becomes of this intention (to take over Rome and the Church) which perhaps holds the key to understanding the poem as a whole and why Arthur fails at the end.

Wyclif argues against revenge and cruelty and argues for the natural order of things. Hence, almost any war is unjust, unsanctioned by God and devoid of correct intention. Throughout the poem knights avenge others, including Arthur himself in killing Mordred, which it is possible to interpret as a fundamental questioning of the legitimacy of war and its deeds. Only God has the right to take life, indeed to avenge sin. In some cases, such as when the 'bowmen of Britain' shoot their arrows causing horses to suffer (lines 2098–2100) or when knights stab horses (1488), a Wycliffite interpretation might suggest that these warriors are even more sinful because in the animal kingdom, warfare does not exist. To sin against innocent animals is an affront to God Himself.

If the poet is expressing Wycliffite sympathies, this could be one of the key explanations for his graphic description of war and its consequences. Certainly, war's horror is everywhere; it is as if we are seeing what can happen when order is disturbed and chaos unleashed. Consequently, the figure of the Giant of Mont Saint Michel, raping women and eating children, might well be a metaphor for the poem as a whole: war has no order, no chivalry, no religion. While Arthur defeats this ghoulish creation in the flesh, his pains are nothing compared to what is to follow. If his intention is to seize Rome, his overweening pride will become his downfall; in his pursuit of an unjust war, he is doomed by God. Lady Fortune's appearance in his second dream, where Arthur rises to the highest level only to be dashed to the ground (lines 3250–3393), delivers a harsh verdict on a king who seeks to follow an unjust path.

Dating the poem

The context and themes discussed above appear to suggest a date for the poem in the latter half of the fourteenth century, with many pointing to the reigns of either Richard II or Henry IV. A broad date can be ascribed to the poem by its descriptions of warfare and placing it within the Alliterative Revival. As seen above, the poem pays strong attention to military detail and as such suggests inspiration from the success of the English in France under Edward III. However, this only suggests a date for the poem somewhere between the Battle of Sluys (1340) and perhaps the Siege of Limoges (1370), the description of which in Froissart's *Chronicles* seems to mirror the horror of the destruction of Metz in the poem. This, combined with some of the descriptions of the armour used by the knights, means that the best we can conclude from the purely military narrative is that the poem was written somewhere between 1340 and 1400.

Equally, the place of *King Arthur's Death* in the Alliterative Revival of the fourteenth and fifteenth centuries is only of general assistance. It is possible after all that this 'revival' is a misnomer and may instead reflect a period in which an oral tradition in alliterative poetry began to be written down in English for the first time. However, the poem's inclusion of the Nine Worthies (see above) means that it cannot be earlier than the *Voeux de Paon* of c.1310. This, combined with a strong reliance on the Galfridian narrative and its drawing of themes from other romances, suggests that the poem is not derived from an oral tradition but instead is an innovative (if derivative) work and the product of a particular time.

In recent years, historians have examined the text in greater detail to try and establish when this may have been. It is thought, for example, that the countries referred to in Lucius' distant empire are derived from those described in a travel memoir purportedly written by a Sir John Mandeville c.1357, establishing that the Arthur poem could not have been written before then. Individual work by both L. D. Benson and Mary Hamel has pushed the date of the poem's composition to the first years of the fifteenth century. It is suggested, for example, that the reference to the Duchess of Brittany as a victim of the Giant of Mont Saint Michel (852) – a name which does not occur in the work's potential sources – would have been an inappropriate or offensive reference after Henry IV married the widow of John IV of Brittany in 1402; placing the writing of the poem in the early years of Henry's reign. Benson draws attention to the poet's reference to (and inferred criticism of) 'the Montagues' (3773), a curious reference to some of Mordred's allies who appear nowhere else in the poem. Assuming that this name was not added by Thornton himself, Benson argues that this refers to the heretical Lollard, Sir John Montagu, a prominent supporter of Richard II, who was executed following the failed Epiphany Plot of 1399–1400. By 1409, the Montagues had been restored to their estates as allies of Henry IV, limiting the writing of the poem to the first decade of the fifteenth century. Benson also suggests that the description of Mordred as Malebranche, the falsely engendered or bastard (4062, 4174), may refer to a contemporary rumour (mentioned in the chronicles of Froissart) that Richard was not the son of Edward, the Black Prince, but instead of a liaison between his mother, Joan of Kent, and a priest. Such rumours may well have been promulgated by supporters of Henry to legitimise his position following his return to England (in the manner of Arthur, indeed) and his usurpation of the crown from Richard in 1399.

In this light, Joan of Kent may be a model for Guinevere. In the poem Guinevere grants Mordred access to Arthur's wardrobe – in effect the office of state – at Wallingford and his ceremonial sword, Clarent (lines 4202–8). Benson suggests that Joan's own residence at Wallingford between 1361 and 1385, combined with contemporary rumours about her perceived licentious behaviour, are used by the poet to imply that Richard II was illegitimate. Joan was married to Sir William Montagu, Second Earl of Salisbury, before that marriage was annulled by the pope on the grounds of her secret marriage (at the age of twelve) to Sir Thomas Holland, which was then reinstated. His death and Joan's subsequent marriage to the Black Prince did little to quell the rumours about her, not least because Montagu himself was still alive and a source of gossip. The poem's reference to Mordred and Guinevere seeking refuge in the west of Britain (Mordred) and the north-west (Guinevere), is a further link between them and Richard, with his interests in Ireland and his supporters in Cheshire. It may well be that the poet, in drawing these parallels and rekindling old rumours, sought to legitimise the claims of Henry IV to the English crown by implying that Richard's own paternal descent could not be proven. In other words, Richard II had no right to the crown of England unlike Henry who, as son of John of Gaunt (brother of Edward III), had cast-iron credentials; that is, Mordred, the Malebranche, might loosely be seen as Richard II, and Arthur as Henry.

Italian politics, in particular those involving the city state of Milan, are also instructive on dating and, though confusing, represent a strong contemporary interest in the region. Benson argues that it was only with the marriage of Lionel Duke of Clarence to Violante, daughter of Galeazzo II of Milan in 1368, that 'many Englishmen knew about northern Italy' and subsequently that Richard II established 'what amounted to an alliance' with the dukedom. The titles of 'Sire of Milan' (3134) and the 'Viscount of Rome' (325 and elsewhere) appear to link the poem to the lives of Bernabò Visconti (who succeeded as sole ruler of Milan in 1378) and that of Giangaleazzo, his successor as 'Sire' (Signore) of Milan until the proper title became 'Duke' in 1395. The poet's reference to Piacenza, Ponte, Pontremoli, Pisa and Pavia (3140–41) are also seen as indicative: Pavia did not come under the control of Milan until 1360; Pisa not until 1399 (i.e. after the title of 'Sire' became redundant). If the inclusion of Pisa in this list of possessions is correct, the poet may have been using the term 'Sire' based on common practice rather than up-to-date information, placing the date of the poem after 1399. Professor P. J. C. Field, on the other hand, suggests the Duke of Milan's offering of 'one million in gold' to Arthur (3144) may have been inspired by the dowry of two million florins paid to Lionel in 1368. This, alongside indications in the poem about warring regions to be avoided, place the writing of the work closer to the wedding of Lionel; perhaps somewhere between 1375 and when Bernabò achieved sole governance of Milan in 1378.

Benson believes the date to be later. He suggests the route taken by Arthur across Europe to Rome – the 'German Way' (down the Rhine to Lucerne and then via the Gotthard Pass) – is very particular and, in the context of recorded English history, unusual. Although it is possible that records are yet to be found of Englishmen making this journey in an earlier period, it is suggested that the poet part-based his description of Arthur's journey on knowledge of that taken by Adam of Usk in 1402 as recorded in his *Chronicon*. It points to the fact that wars in Milan forced Adam to avoid Tuscany and that his route through Italy to Rome was via towns also referred to in the narrative of *King Arthur's Death*. Not only does Arthur take this route but so does Sir Valiant (lines 325–9) when he refers to avenging the Viscount of Rome (possibly a reference to the Visconti) for taking some of his men in Tuscany (suggesting wars in that area to be avoided).

If it is the case that the poet borrows from Adam – or from travellers who drew upon Adam's knowledge – then this, combined with the other factors mentioned above, makes the case for the writing of *King Arthur's Death* in the first decade of the fifteenth century highly compelling: between 1402 (Adam of Usk) and 1409, when the Montagues were brought back into the royal fold. Furthermore, if the poem is accepted as anti-Richard, and was written before Henry's marriage to Joan (1402), the window becomes even narrower: placing the poem between 1400 and 1402. However, if the poet's intimate knowledge of Milanese affairs does suggest an earlier creation, perhaps written in the shadow of Lionel's wedding to Violante and an increased English knowledge of Italian city state diplomacy, then this places the work in the mid-1370s. The challenge for the reader is whether to see the poem as reflective of the legitimacy of Henry's cause (written c.1400) or as a more general work on the probity of kings (written c.1375–78, at the end of the reign of a dotard Edward III and the beginning of the reign of a child king Richard). A third option is that the poem may instead be a product of the 1370s which was then amended at some point before its final transcription by Thornton. Perhaps the best we can say is that the original poem was written somewhere between 1375 and 1402; either way, it was written at a time when the kingdom of England was in a period of great political instability. Weighing all the options in the balance, however, a date of c.1400 remains the most attractive.

The intended audience

What did an early fifteenth-century audience look like? The messages and themes within *King Arthur's Death* are so rich and complex, so multi-layered, that they suggest an intelligent audience. Robert Thornton collected together works which were either secular entertainment, religious or instructive in nature; *King Arthur's Death* falls into the first of these categories. At first glance, the poem gives every appearance of being enjoyed by knights and lords in some chivalric setting, laughing at the brutality, siding with the patriotic thrust, revelling in the chivalric display and martial rigour of the British abroad. Certainly, given the context of the Hundred Years War and England's military malaise under Richard, this is appealing. It is also questionable.

The poem begins with a prayer (lines 4–6), asking God

> ... that by His grace and guidance   we govern ourselves
> In this wretched world,   and through virtuous living
> And care, we reach His court,   the Kingdom of Heaven

The poet appears to be a religious man, not secular in his approach, despite the apparent subject matter of the poem itself. Indeed, it features constant references to God, Christ and Mary; Sir Kay and King Arthur seek confession and Sir Priamus seeks conversion. It is clear that the poet is guided by religious morals and, in his reflection on the brutality of war, invites the reader to see behind the propaganda of the chivalric ideal. Following King Arthur through triumph and then fall, illustrating that all men go the same way, his message appears to be one of persuasion by reflection rather than conversion by didactics. For all his earthly power, Arthur's last words are *In manus tuas Domine, commendo spiritum meo* (Into your hands, Lord, I commend my spirit). Arthur, his grandeur gone, slips into God's judgement. For all its length and magnificent sweep, in this one moment the poem contains all the deep power of Thornton's transcription of *Parlement of the Thre Ages*, which also reflects on the folly and brevity of life as one prepares for death. Certainly, therefore, the Arthur-poem has a spiritual and strong philosophical context.

Yet we must not forget that *King Arthur's Death* contains astonishing contemporary detail of warfare, tactics, geography, international trading routes, sailing and navigation, and even heraldry. It has been argued convincingly (for example by Professor Turville-Petre) that the physical quality of the works of the Alliterative Revival is too inferior to suggest that the poets were themselves aristocratic or were writing for an aristocratic audience. Many of the finest works that survive today have done so not necessarily because of their content but because of their physical quality. Aristocratic collections of this time are defined by beautifully illuminated, bound and handwritten works – usually in French or Latin – kept and bequeathed as statements of knowledge and wealth. The works of the alliterative poets were of a lesser nature and few were illustrated (the illustrations accompanying *Sir Gawain and the Green Knight*, for example, have often been derided). So, while many of the poems of the Revival may possess great literary merit, their manuscripts are not impressive, are less grand; not necessarily the treasured possession of a noble lord. Indeed, we must not forget that these works were not 'published' in the current sense and their use, distribution and reason for survival is a subject for debate. Yet they are rich in message and magisterial in their employment of a blossoming English language, in particular the dialect languages of the English regions; they had a specific purpose and a mission, it would seem. So who was the reader? Who heard the poems being read aloud – and why?

The poet himself was clearly knowledgeable, indeed is almost encyclopaedic. He may have been well travelled, perhaps as a merchant or even acting in some form of ambassadorial role, or was well read. The heraldic references are intriguing; the arms of the Viscount of Valence (lines 2050–57), Sir Priamus (2521–3) and King Arthur himself (3646–51) are discussed from the point of view of someone highly knowledgeable in the use of heraldry in military service. As discussed above, his words may be indicative of a knowledge of wars being fought in Italy (most famously, from an English point of view, by the *condottiero* Sir John Hawkwood [*c*.1323–94]), or of Italian diplomacy in general. If the poet was a merchant or courtly ambassador, he might well have been concerned about the stability of trade and travel in a Europe affected by the Papal Schism, the shadow of the Ottomans and the stability of the Holy Roman Empire.

A counter argument is that the poet borrowed from other works to make his poem more substantial and compelling; we have seen above how the work clearly draws from other works in the canon. However, the poet's knowledge is too vast and realistic to be based wholly on reading the works of others alone, and his rich attention to contemporary detail does suggest the work of someone who is well read and able to substantiate his life experiences by references to other literary sources. Hence, while his framing of the poem within the structure of Geoffrey of Monmouth, and his application of scenes from other Arthurian romances, represent his major structural 'borrowing', it is when he builds on top of this that his 'professional' life becomes apparent. This literary framing appears to act as a springboard for a work focused on Britain (in its loosest sense) and/or England and with patriotic themes (the poem often refers to 'our' knights); the need for a stable country appears core to the poet's beliefs. At the same time, his religious expression and moral nuance also inform us that he is a man of spirituality, concerned for humanity in a world of great international uncertainty.

With his religious framework and a sense for stability, the poet in many ways appears as a quiet man with big thoughts. Yet it would be misleading to assert that he was a revolutionary figure demanding significant change. As Bernard Guenée writes (*States and Rulers in Later Medieval Europe*), even the most violent of mediaeval insurgents 'gave expression to very moderate demands'. Certainly, the *Arthur*-poet is more reflective than radical. It would seem, based on the way he writes and the views he expresses, that he – and his audience – might be compared to the upper-middle classes and businesspeople of today: intelligent and active yet unhappy bystanders to world events, seeking stability and continuity in a time of change. In this light, the audience was not rural, nor was it aristocratic;

instead it comprised groups of cosmopolitan people, intellectuals perhaps, who spanned both these worlds and knew their major players. In many ways, we might see the poet and his audience in a group that we might today call 'social influencers', wielding a power greater perhaps than their own social standing might suggest.

A poem for its time and a poem for today

King Arthur's Death is truly a masterpiece and deserves far greater recognition. At its heart is its focus on the psychology of leaders and the consequences of vanity as the world's events sweep ever onwards. While it draws on mystical themes and touches on magical elements, it is nonetheless an acute observation of the loneliness of kingship and the folly of pride. The magnificent grasp of contemporary detail gives the poem astonishing credibility, grounding its characters in a firm and unquestionable reality which enables us to empathise with their thoughts and feel their inner turmoil. Yet, amid all the action and epic sweep of the narrative, it is the two dream sequences which frame this stunning work and ultimately define its power. The struggle between the dragon and the bear show us a king disturbed by the justice of his actions; the horror of Fortune's Wheel reveals the fragility of a rule gained by overweening pride and brutal destruction. In letting us see Arthur's most private inner doubts in these two startling dreams, the poet shares with us the intimate horror faced by all such leaders: that the real devil comes at night.

Despite its Arthurian conceit, this is a convincing account of what happens when kings – leaders, indeed – come to believe that they alone are right. While the late fourteenth century is its setting, nuanced advice to monarchs its theme, this poem is no mere quaint romance of warriors fighting abstract battles set in a distant world. *King Arthur's Death* is a real work for here and now. In our own time, where populism and nationalist politics appear to offer some glorious short-term escape from a perceived national decline or injustice, the poem is a striking warning to leaders who seek to stoke the flames of nationhood for political ends. *King Arthur's Death* acts as a cautionary tale, revealing in its finale the inevitable consequence of a political vision driven by vanity, pride and revenge. In pursuit of his passion, Arthur turns his country against itself, sees the destruction of his closest friends and, ultimately, in one last desperate battle, is fatally wounded by the blade of Clarent, his own sword of state. *King Arthur's Death* is a powerful argument against the unforeseen repercussions of unshackled political obsession. It asks its audience whether vanity and pride can ever be the substance of kingship, whether war and bloodshed can ever rightly be the tools of justice, and whether it is ever legitimate to sacrifice all for an illusory gain. It is as relevant today as six centuries ago.

THE STORY

The poem can be divided approximately into four distinctive parts which build to create a compelling overall narrative and meaning to the work. The first section (1–1221) begins with Arthur holding Christmas at Carlisle when the enjoyment of the festivities is spoiled by the arrival of Roman emissaries who demand that the king pays homage for his lands to Sir Lucius, the Emperor of Rome. Annoyed, Arthur takes advice from his lords and prelates and sends the emissaries back to Rome stating that, on the contrary, Rome should pay homage to him. Now Arthur builds an army and sails to France, leaving Mordred in charge of the kingdom. On his way, he is disturbed by a dream of a battle between a dragon and a bear; his sages tell him that the victory of the dragon signals Arthur's victory against Lucius. His arrival in France is marked by doing battle with the fearsome Giant of Mont Saint Michel, whose defeat closes the first section, which sets the psychological, ethical and military scene for what is to follow.

In the second section (1222–2370), we follow a largely martial narrative with decisions taken based on conventional military and legal bases. When Arthur learns of the emperor Lucius' advance towards him, he despatches Sir Gawain to advise Lucius to leave his lands. His refusal, followed by Gawain beheading the emperor's uncle for his contemptuous words, leads to the Romans pursuing the Britons and capturing Sir Boice. In renewed fighting, Sir Boice is rescued and Senator Peter, the Roman battle leader, is captured and sent captive to Paris with a number of his lords. Lucius dispatches a force to rescue the senator but his ambush party ultimately fails, despite causing some casualties to the British force led by Sir Cador. Finally, the two armies meet at Soissons; in a ferocious battle, Sir Kay is slain and his death is avenged by Arthur who eventually kills Sir Lucius. The Roman baggage train is then looted and Arthur sends the enemy dead back to Rome with a message telling the city that their dead shall be the only tribute they receive from him. Whilst at his most victorious, we now see the seeds of pride start to grow in Arthur.

The tone of the poem changes dramatically in the third section (2371–3205) as Arthur begins to change from 'Just War' king to a man driven by pride and revenge. Expressing an interest in the renown of the Duke of Lorraine, perhaps fearful of him within his realms or seeing him as a thorn in his side as he advances on Rome, Arthur lays siege to the city of Metz. Sir Gawain and a force of foragers are sent into the hills where they meet the mysterious Sir Priamus, apparently loyal to Lorraine. Gawain and Priamus battle almost to the death before Gawain beats his rival, who changes sides and seeks to convert to Christianity. Eventually, in a manner reminiscent of Jean Froissart's description of the Siege of Limoges (1370), Metz falls to a devastating assault although, in a nod to the chivalric ideal, Arthur spares the Duchess of Lorraine, in addition to the women, children and non-combatant inhabitants. The Duke of Lorraine is sent to England to end his days in captivity. Now Arthur is free to march on Rome, crossing the Alps in the manner of Hannibal and taking Como before descending into Tuscany. Arthur is greeted by a cardinal who pleads with him, promising Arthur the Roman crown while leaving the king with noble hostages as surety.

On the eve of his greatest triumph at the opening of the fourth section (3206–4346), at the height of his powers, Arthur has the second of his dreams; this one in stark contrast to the first. Now he meets with Lady Fortune who lures him towards her terrible wheel. Here he meets eight (he himself is the ninth) of the Nine Worthies, six of whom have already fallen from the wheel. Believing he will be raised to the wheel's summit, he is instead thrown crashing down from it, and wakes from his dream to be advised by his sages that his finest days are over; he must repent of his sins and prepare for his end. Walking alone, he meets with Sir Craddock, on pilgrimage from Britain, who tells Arthur that Mordred has seized the kingdom, taken Guinevere as his wife and has children by her. Arthur now returns to Britain and wins a fierce battle off the coast before Gawain, landing impetuously, is overwhelmed by Mordred's forces and killed by Mordred himself who, on discovering whom he has killed, is filled with remorse. Eventually, King Arthur lands and finds the bodies of Gawain and his men; filled with grief, he vows revenge, taking his forces westwards beyond the river Tamar to battle with Mordred. Here, though outnumbered, his army fights valiantly and Arthur slays Mordred although not without cost; he, too, is mortally wounded and many of his most loyal knights lose their lives. Mordred's army is wiped out but Arthur, and all his grandeur, is reduced to naught; he asks to be taken to Glastonbury to be buried. Guinevere is confined to a convent and her children ordered slain; the kingdom itself is to be handed to Arthur's blood-cousin, Constantine. Finally, Arthur confesses his sins and forgives those who have wronged him.

NOTES ON THIS TRANSLATION

The original manuscript in Middle English for the *Alliterative Morte Arthure*, as transcribed by Edmund Brock in the nineteenth century, has an astonishing pace and rhythm. This makes it a fundamentally vibrant text with a distinct voice which I wished to maintain. I have had to focus on a variety of different aspects to maintain authenticity: accurate tense and punctuation, a contemporary vocabulary and appropriate alliteration. These elements, combined with an understanding of the period in which the poem was written, also played a key role in how I chose to illustrate it, as explained below.

Tense and punctuation

I have maintained wherever possible the tense of the words used by the poet. This gives a greater flow and also a greater urgency to the work, particularly when read aloud, e.g. when Arthur dies, he 'speaks no more', rather than 'he spoke no more'.

I have also inserted a caesura in each line to facilitate the flow and to create the feel of how the poem would originally have been read. This may not be a requirement but those wishing to read the poem aloud will be assisted by this; it also enables the reader to understand where a particular emphasis lies.

Wherever possible, apostrophes are avoided by careful phrasing. The manuscript implies their use (e.g. *the kingez chamber*) but does not employ them. However, for poetic flow, I have used them on rare occasions. For example, 'For dread of some dog's son in yonder dim bushes' (line 1723) would otherwise be clumsy: 'For the dread of some son of a dog in yonder dim bushes'. This seems an acceptable compromise.

Vocabulary

My choice of words has been driven wherever possible to reflect the brevity of the original form and its rattling alliteration. I have chosen to avoid words which, when translated, would not have existed, etymologically, around the time of the poem. However, some words which date to the later Middle Ages have been included if they create a contemporary effect. Modern words, by which I mean those created in more recent times and whose origins stem back to the 1800s, have been avoided (although I am sure someone will find examples!). In some cases I have retained words which I believe have a particular power even though today their use is tamer. For example, the word *towche*, used by the poet to describe how weapons pierce the inner organs of the body. By translating it, correctly, as 'touch', I have intended to convey the insidious nature of how a large bladed weapon does its worst damage by dint of its slightest and largely unseen impact (e.g. severing an artery or reaching the brain).

Alliterative method

In view of all the above, the alliteration of the original poem has thrown up a series of challenges. To compound these, I have chosen wherever possible to adhere to the alliterative sound intended by the poet.

If a letter at the beginning of a word is alliterated, I have tried to follow that (e.g. line 622):

> *Drawes in by Danuby,   and dubbez hys knyghtez*
> And draws in by the Danube   and dubs his new knights

If a letter is the alliterative intent but does not necessarily appear at the beginning of the word, I have tried to follow that (e.g. line 13, where the letter or sound of 'd' is alliterated):

> *Off elders of alde tyme   and of their awke dedys*
> Of elders of old times   and of their wondrous deeds,

Sometimes, it is difficult to find the alliteration with words which begin with the same letter as used by the poet. In these cases, I have chosen words where the alliterative letter is still maintained by emphasis, even though it does not appear at the beginning of the word (e.g. the word 'speaks', for *karpes*, and 'encouragement' for *corage* in line 1725):

> And with <u>c</u>orage <u>k</u>ene   he <u>k</u>arpes thes wordes
> And with <u>k</u>een en<u>c</u>ouragement,   he spea<u>k</u>s these words

Sometimes, the poet alliterates on a combination of letters and here I have followed that (e.g. line 1717):

> Whedyre we <u>sch</u>one or <u>sch</u>ewe,   <u>sch</u>yft as the lykes.
> Whether we <u>sh</u>un or <u>sh</u>ow;   we will <u>sh</u>ift as you wish

If the poet was alliterating sounds, but it is not possible to replicate the alliteration conventionally because a modern word does not exist, I have used words which, by their pronunciation, replicate the intended alliteration (e.g. line 3843):

> He <u>sch</u>are hyme one the <u>sch</u>orte rybbys   a <u>sch</u>aftmonde large!
> He <u>sh</u>ears him deep in the <u>sh</u>ort ribs   by <u>s</u>urely a hand-span!

A particular feature of the poem is that some alliteration (either of letter or sound) carries on for several lines (e,g, the alliteration on 'f' in lines 2483–92) . In these cases, I have also followed the poet even when, at times, it has tested every cavern of my intellect! This curious feature, in addition to varying dialect usage, has led to the suggestion that the original poem may have been written by two different people, although I am unconvinced.

General layout

The original poem is written as one continuous work, broken up by illuminated letters and also divided into sections of varying line lengths. To help readers using Brock's *Alliterative Morte Arthure* and other editions, I have numbered the lines by every fifth line. In terms of the divisions of the poem, this is open to speculation. I have followed the guidance contained within the original poem, as highlighted by Brock, in which illuminated letters appear at the beginning of some sections. I have created a series of linocut illuminated letters, based on the standardised letter form of the Macclesfield alphabet, and have used these to create the appropriate breaks in the poem. I have also followed the text divisions shown in Brock (which do not carry illuminated letters), in addition to those suggested by Benson and Krishna, where appropriate.

Lines and line sequence

Robert Thornton may be described as a non-professional copyist and it is possible (but not necessarily so) that he made a number of scribal errors throughout his transcription of the work. In 1937, E. V. Gordon and E. Vinaver compared the *Alliterative Morte Arthure* manuscript to that of Malory's *Le Morte D'Arthur*, which uses the poem as a source. They revealed that Malory (in the 'Winchester Manuscript', the only surviving manuscript copy of his great work and written within ten years of his death in 1471) was using a different version of the poem than that contained in the Thornton manuscript. Indeed, the poem may once have been longer, with many lines excluded by Thornton for reasons now unknown. Hence, the arrangement of some of the lines in Brock has been challenged by L. D. Benson and others. For example, Benson, following Gordon and Vinaver, has incorporated two new lines not contained within Brock. I am not entirely convinced they are necessary but have left them in with their own line marked next to them (lines 769a and 771b) and italicised the text. However, for clarity, I have chosen not to add further lines suggested by Gordon and Vinaver and others. In so doing, and to ensure consistency with Brock, all other lines retain the standard numbering.

Later in the poem, I have retained Brock's original line sequence (lines 3068–83) after the Siege of Metz rather than changing the sequence in the manner of both S. Armitage and B. Stone (who, following Benson, move these lines to appear after line 3111, and alter the preceding line sequence). While this makes sense and may support the view that Thornton made scribal errors (the lines can appear at odds with the previous description of the end of the siege), an adherence to Brock does not create too great a distortion of the poem and the section is still comprehensible in the sweep of the action. To my mind these lines are better attributed to the aftermath of the Metz siege, invoking as they do the sheer terror of a civilian population.

To help the reader, a detailed glossary is provided at the end, in addition to a selection of notes (indicated by a dagger shape on the relevant lines) to explain historical nuances within the text. Throughout, I have retained the use of British imperial measurements wherever they occur in the manuscript and have used these also in the notes and glossary. A conversion guide from imperial to metric is supplied at the end of the glossary.

The Illustrations

When I began work on this magnificent poem, I intended to illustrate it with a distinctive set of pen-and-ink drawings to evoke the sense of a mediaeval manuscript. I quickly realised that this would be insufficient to support a poem which carries so many textured layers, not least of which is an underlying critique of chivalry, a probing assessment of the validity of war and an incredibly dark sense of humour. For a while I was troubled by how to proceed, but during the process, I studied the work of the German artist and printmaker Käthe Kollwitz. I realised that the darkness of what she had observed, in terms of the horrors of war, set the right tone for this translation. Hence, you will see the influence of Kollwitz in many of the illustrations; my hope is that this achieves two key objectives: to point new admirers in the direction of her work and, from my point of view, to substantiate the *Arthur*-poet's intent in writing this stunning work. Having said this, you will see that some of the illustrations are more akin to my work in *Sir Gawain and the Green Knight*. This has also been deliberate; in contrasting a more naïve style with that of Kollwitz, I wanted also to reveal what I think is a key intention of the original *Arthur*-poet: that chivalry and romance are one thing and the foul reality of war another.

Michael Smith, April 2020

King Arthur's Death

The Alliterative Morte Arthure

Here begins Morte Arthure. In Nomine Patris
et Filii et Spiritus Sancti. Amen pur Charite. Amen †

Now great glorious God,   through the grace of Himself
And the precious prayers   of His priceless Mother,
Shield us from sinful works   and from a shameful death,
So that by His grace and guidance   we govern ourselves
    In this wretched world,   and through virtuous living 5
And care, we reach His court,   the Kingdom of Heaven,
When our souls shall part   asunder from the body,
Ever to be and bide   in bliss with Himself;
And show me how to weave   some words at this time,
That be neither void nor vain   but will venerate Him, 10
And which will please and profit   all people who hear them.

You who likes to listen,   or who loves to hear,
Of elders of old times   and of their wondrous deeds,
How they were loyal to their religion,   and loved God almighty,
Harken high unto me   and hold yourself still 15
And I shall tell you a tale   that is both true and noble
Of the royal ranks   of the Round Table
Who were champions of chivalry,   the choicest of chieftains,
Both cautious in their works   and wise men of arms,
Doughty in their doings,   and dreading of shame, 20
Kind men and courteous,   knowing of courtly ways;
How they won through warring   much wondrous honour,
Slew Lucius the loathsome   that was lord of Rome,
And conquered his kingdom   through craft of arms;
Harken now hitherward   and hear this story! † 25

When that King Arthur   had won back by conquest
Many castles and kingdoms   and countless lands,
He had reclaimed completely   the crown of those countries
That were controlled by Uther   in his time on earth: †
    Argyle and Orkney   and all those outer isles; 30
Ireland utterly,   fully circled by sea;
Mischievous Scotland   he commands with skill;
And Wales, by war,   he won at his will;

31

Both Flanders and France   he holds freely himself;
Holland and Hainault   were both held by him too;   35
Burgundy, Brabant   and Brittany no less;
Guyenne and Gotland   and noble Grasse; †
Bayonne and Bordeaux,   he built most fair,
Touraine and Toulouse   with towers full high;
Poitiers and Provence,   he held as their prince;   40
And Valence and Vienne,   of most noble value,
And Auvergne and Anjou,   those very rich earldoms;
By conquest full cruel,   they knew him as lord
Of Navarre and Norway,   and Normandy too,
Of Germany and Austria   and others enough;   45
He dominates Denmark   through dread of himself
From Swynn into Sweden   with his swiping sword! †

When these deeds he had done,   he dubbed his knights,
Dispersed and dealt dukedoms   in diverse realms;
Made of his cousins   great anointed kings,   50
Bearing the crowns   of those kingdoms they coveted.
When he had ridden these realms   and ruled the people,
That royal one rested   and held the Round Table;
He stays all that season   at his own leisure
Abroad in Great Britain,   as he liked the best;   55
Then went into Wales   with his fellows too,
Sways into South Wales   with his swift hounds,
To go hunting for harts   in the high lands
In Glamorgan with glee,   and eternal gladness.
And there he founds a city   by assent of his lords   60
Which was called Caerleon,   with curious walls, †
On that rich river   which runs so fair,
So he might see as he wished   his court all assembled.

Then after, at Carlisle,   Christmas he keeps,
This self-same Conqueror,   where they held him as lord, †   65
With dukes and his Dozen Peers   of diverse realms, †
Earls and archbishops,   and others enough,
Bishops and bachelors   and noble baronets,
Who bow to his banner   and do his bidding:

32

And on Christmas Day,   when they were assembled,   70
That comely Conqueror,   he commands himself
That each lord should linger   and not take his leave,
Till the tenth day was taken   in full to its end.
Thus in royal array   he held his Round Table,
With spectacle and splendour   and sumptuous meats;   75
There was never such grandeur   in the whole time of man
As made in midwinter   in the West March! †

But on New Year's Day,   at noon precisely,
As the boldest at the board   were served of their bread,
So suddenly entered   a Senator of Rome,   80
With some sixteen knights   serving him as his escort.
He saluted the sovereign,   and also that hall,
As king to a king,   and made bows inclining; †
Guinevere in her degree   he greeted as he pleased
And bowed again to the King   to give him this message: 85
'Sir Lucius Iberius,   the Emperor of Rome,
Salutes you as subject,   under his great seal, †
As credentials, Sir King,   with its commanding words,
That this is truly no trifle,   as his arms attest! †
Now on this New Year,   as signed here by notables,   90
I summon you in this hall   to sue for your lands,
That on Lammas day,   and with no let or hindrance, †
You be ready at Rome   with all your Round Table,
And appear in his presence   with all your prized knights
At the Prime of the day,   on pain of your lives,   95
In that acclaimed Capitol   before my King himself,
When he and his Senators   will be sat as they like
To hear you answer alone   why you hold the lands
That owe homage to him   and his elders of old;
Why you have raided and robbed   and ransomed the people   100
And cut down his cousins,   all anointed kings.
There you shall give reckoning   for all your Round Table;
Why you rebel against Rome   and withhold your rents!
If you refuse this summons,   he sends you these words:
He shall seek you over the sea   with sixteen kings,   105
Burn all of Great Britain   and butcher your knights

And bring you back as a beast,   begging to breathe,
And not to rest nor repose   under rich heaven
That for fear of Rome   you are run to ground!
For if you flee into France   or Friesland either   110
You shall be fetched with force   and overthrown for ever!
Your father made fealty,   we find in our rolls
In the register of Rome,   as looks so right;
Without further trifling,   we ask for the tribute
That was won by Julius Ceasar   with his gentle knights!'   115

The King blackly looks   with broad eyes on that noble,
That boiled bright with anger   and burned just like coals;
They cast colours so cruel   across his kingly features
That he looked like a lion   and bites on his lip!
   The Romans for dread   hurled themselves to the earth   120
For fear of his face,   just as if they were dead:
Quivering like kennets,   in front of the king;
Just one look at his countenance   made them contrite!
Then, clearly, a cowering knight   stood up and cried:
'King crowned by accord,   courteous and noble,   125
Harm not the messenger   but mind to your honour
Since we move at your whim   and beseech your mercy;
We belong to Sir Lucius   that is lord of Rome,
The most marvellous man   who roams all the earth,
And we lawfully work   to please him as he wills;   130
We come at his command,   you must please excuse us.'

Then the Conqueror speaks   these cruel words:
'Ha! Craven knight,   a coward you seem!
There is one supreme in this hall   who is sorely grieved
That you dare not for all Lombardy   look on him once!'   135
'Sire,' says the Senator.   'So may Christ help me –
The violence of your visage   has vanquished us all!
You are the most lordly lord   that I ever looked on.
I do not lie when I tell you   that you seem like a lion!'
'You have summoned me,' said the King   'and said what you like.   140
For the sake of your sovereign   I have suffered to hear you;
Since I was crowned in this country   and anointed with chrism,

34

The Romans for dread   hurled themselves to the earth
For fear of his face,   just as if they were dead

Was there never a creature   that spoke so big to me!
But I shall take counsel   from my kings anointed,
From my dukes, leading lords   and well-read theologians,   145
From the peers of my parliament,   from prelates and others,
And the most regal ranks   of the Round Table;
Then I shall take advice   of valiant nobles,
And follow the wisdom   of my wisest knights.
To talk wasteful words   bestows on me no honour   150
Nor does wreaking revenge   when acting through wrath. †

Therefore you shall stay here   and lodge with these lords
These seven nights in pleasure   to rest all your horses
And see what lives we lead here   in these humble lands.'
So for this royalty of Rome,   that richest of states,   155
He commands Sir Kay: 'Take care of these lords,
Attend to these stout men   as custom demands;
Make haste now to house them   in our highest chambers,
And thence in our halls   be they suitably served;
See they find no fault   in the food for their horses;   160
Nor want for wine nor wax candle   nor wealth in this land;
And spare naught on spices   but spend what you like
That there be largesse unlimited   and no lacking found;
Wait on them to my honour   and why, on my word,
I will grant you great gifts   that shall gain you for ever!'   165

Now they are housed as behoves,   beheld highly as guests,
With haste and homage   within these high walls.
In chambers with chimneys   they change their clothes
Until the chancellor fetched them   with chivalrous knights;
Soon the Senator was sat,   as befitting his status,   170
With the king at his table;   two knights courtly served him
With as singular reverence   as Arthur himself,
Richly on his right hand   at the Round Table; †
For the Romans were reasoned   as richly regarded,
And of the most royal blood   that reigned on earth.   175

Then in comes the first course   and placed before the king:
Boar-heads that were brightly   burnished with silver,
Served by trained and taught men,   all richly attired,
Servants of royal blood,   some sixty at once;
Fattened flesh of the season,   with noble frumenty,   180
And all the game you would want for,   and wonderful birds,
Peacocks and plovers   on platters of gold,
Piglets of porcupine   that had never seen pasture,
Then herons by their plumage   hidden full fair,
Great swans full displayed   on silver chargers,   185
Tarts made from turkey   to taste when they liked,
Gumbalds most gorgeous,   gracious to the taste,

Broad shoulders of boar,   the best flesh true sliced,
Barnacle geese and bittern,   battered in dishes,
And young hobbies in bread,   nothing tasted better,   190
With breast of barrow,   the brightest to be seen;
Then come several stews   most joyously after
In an azure sauce,   that seemed all aflame;
And from the jelly of which   flares leapt high aloft
To delight every lord   that would look upon them.   195
Then cranes and curlews   roasted with craft,
Coneys in spiced cream   coloured most fair,
And pheasants enfolded   in flaming silver,
Adorned with many dainties   and daubed with egg;
Then Claret and Cretan wine   cleverly run   200
Through most curious conduits   all of clear silver;
Alsace and Algarve wine   and many others;
Rochelle and Rhenish wine –   none was ever richer –
Vernage from Venice,   with the virtues of Crete,
From taps of fine gold   that flowed on demand.   205
The cupboard of the king   enclosed all his silver,
With great gold-gilt goblets   of glorious hues;
And there was a chief butler,   a most noble chevalier,
Sir Kay the courteous   who served from one cup †
A set of sixty cups more   made for the King's company,   210
Skilfully crafted   and curved with great beauty,
Each one partly picked out   with precious stones
That no poison should slip   secretly past them †
Lest the bright gold beneath   should burst it all asunder
And the venom be void   by virtue of those stones.   215
The Conqueror himself   was likewise cleanly arrayed,
Clad in colours of clear gold,   with his company of knights,
Dressed with his diadem   on his great dais,
For he was deemed the doughtiest   that dwelt on earth.

Then the Conqueror kindly   spoke to those lords   220
And cheered the Romans   with right royal speech:
'Sirs, be knightly of countenance   and comfort yourselves;
We know naught in this country   of curious meats,
In these barren lands   breeds no such thing,

So without feigning pleasure,   please force this food down   225
And feed yourselves with such feeble fare   as you find before you.' †
'Sir,' says the Senator,   'so help me Christ,
Such royalty never reigned   within the walls of Rome!
There is no prelate, nor Pope,   nor prince on this earth
That would not be well pleased   with this precious food!'   230

 As was due by their rank,   they wash and walked the room,
This well-acclaimed Conqueror   with countless of his knights;
Sir Gawain the worthy leads   Guinevere on one side,
On the other was Sir Uhtred,   the Lord of Turin.
    Then thereafter they spent   spices unsparingly; †   235
Then Malmsey and Muscatel,   those marvellous drinks,
Were served round most quickly   in russet-gold cups
To all those rich ones in turn,   the Romans as well.
Then that sovereign, in truth,   as pleased himself,
Assigned to the Senator   certain great lords   240
To lead him to his lodgings,   when he asks for his leave,
With mirth and sweet melody   of noble minstrels.
Then the Conqueror afterwards   goes to take counsel
With lords whose allegiance   is owed to himself;
Joyfully he wends   to the Giant's Tower †   245
With justices, judges   and gentle knights.

Sir Cador of Cornwall   speaks to the King,
Looking on him with love,   and likeably laughs:
'I thank God for that trouble   that thus threatens us!
You will be hard tried I think   lest you teach them better!   250
That letter of Sir Lucius   lightens my heart;
We have lived as wastrels   for many a long day
With delights in this land,   and in many lordships,
And lessened the lauding   of our noble esteem.
I blush red, by our Lord,   for our best nobility   255
Grown sad for disuse   of their deeds in arms!
Now wakens the war!   Let Christ be worshipped!
We will win back renown   by our valour and strength!' †

'Sir Cador,' said the King,   'Your counsel is noble,
You are magnificent, man,   with your merry words!   260
Yet you heed not the context   nor consider the consequence,
And let your hot head speak   as so ruled by your heart!
So I treat you to stay calm,   touching what you say,
And first talk through these tidings   which torment my mind.
You see that the Emperor   is angered somewhat;   265
It seems from his messenger   that he is sorely grieved;
His senator has summoned me   and spoke with contempt,
All haughty in my hall   with his hateful words,
And with despising speech   and sparing me little;
I might not speak for spitting,   my heart is so troubled!   270
He asks as a tyrant   for my tribute to Rome,
Which tearfully was taken   in the time of my elders;
Then, absent aliens   took from us, weak in arms,
What accrued from our commons   as the chronicles tell.
Yet I too have title   to tributes of Rome;   275
My ancestors were emperors   and owned that place also!
Belinus and Brennius   and Baldwin the Third: †
They occupied the Empire   for nigh on eight score winters,
One heir after the other   as old men tell;
They conquered the Capitol   and cast down its walls,   280
Hanged all of their head men,   a hundred at once,
Then Constantine our kinsman   conquered it after, †
Who was heir to England,   and Emperor of Rome,
He that captured the true Cross,   by craft of arms,
On which Christ was crucified   who is King of Heaven.   285
So we too ask for evidence,   the same as the Emperor:
By what right he claims   to be ruler of Rome?'

Then King Angus answered   to Arthur himself,
'You ought to be overlord   of all other kings,
The most wise and worthy   and weightiest of hand,   290
And most knightly in counsel   that ever wore crown!
     I do say for Scotland   that we suffered loss
When those Romans reigned   and ransomed our elders
And rode in a riot   and ravished our wives,
Without reason or right   robbing us of our goods;   295

39

So I shall make my vow   devoutly to Christ
And the holy Vernicle,   virtuous and noble,
That for this great villainy   I will now take revenge
On those venomous men   with my valiant knights!
I shall furnish trained forces   for your defence;   300
Fifty thousand men,   within two months, †
Paid from my own pocket   to wend where you like
And fight with your foes   that treat us unfairly!'

Then that bold noble,   the lord of Brittany,
Counsels King Arthur   and calls on him   305
To answer those aliens   with audacious words
And entice the Emperor   to travel over the mountains.
          He said, 'I make my vow,   vehemently to Christ
And the holy Vernicle: I will never leave your side
For fear of no Roman   that reigns on earth: 310
We will always be ready,   found in battle array,
And no more dubious of dents   from their deadly weapons
Than of the dew that is damp   when it drops to earth,
And no more shy of the sweep   of their sharpest swords
Than as if they were flowers   grown fresh in the field!   315
I will bring surely to battle   my best knights in byrnies,
Thirty thousand by tally,   a throng fully armed,
Within a month and a day   to whichever land
That you thus seek to send them   as when you think best.'

'Ay, Ay!' says the Welsh king,   'let Christ be worshipped! †   320
Now shall we wreak full well   the wrath of our elders!
In West Wales I know   such horrors they wrought
That all for sorrow they weep   who do dwell on war.
Every man in the vanguard,   I shall have in my charge †
Until I have vanquished   the Viscount of Rome,   325
That wrought me great villainy   at Viterbo once
As I passed on a pilgrimage   by Pontremoli. †
He was in Tuscany then   and took some of our knights,
Arrested them without right   and ransomed them later.
I shall surely ensure   we shall not be reconciled   330
Lest we durst assemble   by ourselves alone

40

And deal dents of death   with our deadly weapons!
So for that war I will fund   my own worshipful knights,
The best warriors of Wales   and the West Marches;
Two thousand in total,   all horsed on steeds,   335
The strongest who I know   in all those west lands!'

Sir Ewain Fitz Urien   then full eagerly asks,
He who was the king's kinsman   and courageous himself,
'Sir, if we would know your will,   we would do what you
     wish;
Whether we journey now   or adjourn until later,   340
To ride on those Romans   and ravage their lands,
We are shaped to ship   to go when you wish.'

'Kinsman,' said the Conqueror,   'you ask most kindly
If my counsel accords   so to conquer those lands;
Come then the first day of June,   we shall quickly engage them   345
With our cruellest knights,   so may Christ comfort me!
Therefore unto Christ   I make this vow devoutly,
And to the holy Vernicle,   virtuous and noble:
I shall at Lammas take leave   to long at my will
In Lorraine or Lombardy,   wherever I like;   350
To march on to Milan   and mine down the walls
Of Pietrasanta and Pisa   and of Pontremoli;
In the Vale of Viterbo   I will victual my knights,
Stay there for six weeks   and refresh myself;
Send knights to that prized city,   and plant my siege at that place, 355
Unless they proffer peace   in appropriate time.' †

'For certain,' says Sir Ewain,   'and so I now avow,
That may I ever see that man   with my own eyes
That squats in your birthright,   the Empire of Rome,
I shall chance at once   to snatch at his eagle,   360
That is borne on his banner   of bright rich gold,
And wrench it from his retinue   and rive it asunder
Lest it be readily rescued   by his riotous knights! †
I shall reinforce those you field   with fresh men-at-arms –
Fifty thousand fine men   all on fair steeds –   365

41

To fall on your foe   as you would see fit
In France or in Friesland   to fight where you will!'

'By Our Lord,' said Sir Lancelot,   'now this lifts my heart!
I laud God for the love   these lords have avowed!
Now may lesser men please   also say what they like   370
With no let to hold them,   but first listen to me:
I shall be there to join battle,   with my most gentle knights,
On a jaunty steed   so joyously girded,
Just as that day starts   to joust with Sir Lucius,
Among all his giants,   those Genoese also, †   375
And strike him stiff from his steed,   with the strength of my hands,
Despite all those strongmen   that stand with him there!
With all my retinue arrayed,   I reckon it but little effort
To make my road to Rome   with my riotous knights!
So in seven whole days   with six score knights   380
I shall be ready at sea   to sail when you like!'

Then Sir Lot laughs   and speaks loudly to all:
'I like it that Sir Lucius   does long for sorrow;
Now he wants for war   so his woes begin;
It is our fate to wreak   all the wrath of our fathers!   385
I make my vow to God   and the holy Vernicle
That if I see the Romans   who are so held with renown,
Arrayed in their armour   on the field all around,
I shall for the reverence   of the Round Table
Ride all through their army,   its rear guard and battles, †   390
Making ready ways   with room through those ranks,
That will run with red blood   as my steed rushes!
And he that follows my faring,   and comes first after me,
Shall find in my footsteps   my foe dead and fallen!'

Then the Conqueror kindly   comforts these knights   395
And lauds them all greatly   and most lordly avows:
'May all-wielding God   worship you all;
Let me not want for others   while I reign in this world!
For my esteem and manhood   you maintain on earth,
And all my honour completely,   where other kings rule;   400

My wealth and the worship   of all this rich world
Has come from your conquests   to ennoble my crown!
He need fear for no foes   who leads such folk,
Always fresh for more fighting   in the field at the ready!
I cower before no king   that lives under Christ;   405
While I see you all sound,   no one shall beset me!'

 With their talking completed,   then trumpets blew;
Thus those dukes and earls   descended to dance
And in that hall they assembled   and so supped together,
All these seemly lords,   with most noble splendour.   410
Then that right royal king   charms all these knights
With a riotous revelling   of all his Round Table,
Till seven days had passed,   when the Senator asks,
With audacious words: What shall the Emperor be told?

After Epiphany,   with his proposals discussed   415
By peers of the parliament,   prelates and others,
The King in his council room,   courteous and noble,
Calls for those Romans   and replies by himself:
'Greet well Lucius, your lord,   do not lessen these words:
If you be loyal liegemen   let him know soon   420
I shall at Lammas take leave   and lodge at my will
At leisure in his lands   with my lords a-plenty,
And reign as their ruler   taking rest where I like;
By the river of Rhône   I will hold my Round Table, †
And seize the funds, by my faith,   of all those fair realms,   425
No matter his might nor his menace   nor contempt in his eyes!
And I will march over the mountains   into his main lands,
To Milan most marvellous,   and mine down its walls; †
And neither shall I leave,   in Lorraine nor Lombardy,
No noble alive   who keeps his laws there;   430
And turn towards Tuscany   when I think it time,
And ride all those broad lands   with my red-blooded knights.
Bid him rescue himself   for the sake of his honour,
And meet me for his manhood   in his home lands!
I shall be found in France,   at his first asking!   435
The first day of February   in those fair marches!

Unless by force I be fetched   and forfeit my lands,
The flower of his fair folk   shall be full left for dead!
He can rest assured,   under my rich seal,
That I will lay siege to Rome   within seven winters   440
And so securely besiege him   upon every side
That many a senator   shall sigh for my sake!
My summons are certain   so I serve to you
Documents of safe conduct   to carry as you please;
I assign lodgings at stages   to rest on your journey   445
From this place to the port   from whence you shall depart:
Seven days to Sandwich   is all I suffer to grant you; †
Sixty miles in a day,   so you have not much time!
You must speed at your spurs   and spare not your horse;
You must wend by Watling Street   and no other way; †   450
You must spend the night   as needs must where you stop;
Be it forest or field,   do not fare from the road;
Bind your horse by a bush   even with its bridle;
Lodge yourself below trees   as you likely think best;
For I will not allow aliens   to amble at night –   455
Above all, not your troop   roaming free to cause riot.
Your licence is limited,   as witnessed by these lords;
Like or loathe it,   I leave that to you,
For both your life and your limb   rely upon this:
Though Sir Lucius claims my lands   owe lordship to Rome,   460
If you are found with one foot   on this side of the sea
Afterwards, on the eighth day,   by when undern rings,
We will behead you with haste   and draw you with horses
And then hang you high   for the hounds to gnaw on!
And all the rents and red gold   that belongs to Rome   465
Will not readily, Sir,   be enough for your ransom!'

'Sir,' says the Senator,   'as Christ may help me,
If I might with honour   at once win away,
I should for no emperor   that lives upon earth
Come again unto Arthur   bearing such a message;   470
But alas, I am here   with just sixteen knights
And beseech you, Sir,   that we may pass safely.
If some lawless man   delays us on our travels

While licenced by you, Lord,   your lustre is tarnished.'
'Worry not,' said the King,   'your conduct is confirmed   475
From Carlisle to the coast,   where your cog waits;
And though your coffers be full,   and crammed all with silver,
My seal would keep you safe   for sixty miles more!'
They inclined low to the King   and politely craved leave
To go quick from Carlisle,   and they take their horses;   480
Sir Cador the courteous,   acquainted well with those roads,
Conveys them to Catterick,   and commends them to Christ.

Then they sped at their spurs,   and made their mounts spring so fast
That they had to hire hastily   fresh horses thereafter.
Thus with rigour they rode   and never rested,   485
Save to lodge below lindens   when the light failed;
And so truly that Senator   sought the quickest way,
With seven days done   they reached that city;
For all the glee under God   they were never so glad
Of the sound of the sea   and the bells of Sandwich!   490
Without stopping for breath,   they stabled horses aboard
And all weary they went   to that wan sea at once.
With all men on board,   the ship weighed its anchors
And rowed fleet on the flood   of high tide towards Flanders †
And through Flanders they fared,   as they thought most fitting,   495
To Aachen in Germany,   in the lands of Arthur,
Going by Mount Gotthard   by most grievous ways, †
And so into Lombardy,   which they liked to see!
They turn into Tuscany   with its soaring towers;
Then appropriately changed   into precious apparel: 500
On Sunday at Sutri   they rest their steeds
And seek the saints of Rome,   to which all knights assented.
Then they spur to the palace   with its splendid portals,
Where Sir Lucius awaits   with his lords a-plenty,
And bow low to him lovingly,   bearing their letters   505
With enclosed credentials   in chivalric words.

Then all eager, the Emperor   enquires with ardour
Of an answer from Arthur;   he asks him right there
How he orders his realm   and rules his people,

And if rebellious against Rome   by what rights he claims this.   510
'You should have seized his sceptre   and sat above him,
Asserting the royalty   of most noble Rome
For you are surely my messenger,   a Senator of Rome;
He should have, out of deference,   submitted to you!'

 'He will bow to no man,   no matter how wealthy,   515
Save to he who would beat him   with warlike strength;
Many will fall first,   left dead on the field,
Before he appears in this place,   despite all of your pressing.
I say, Sir, that Arthur   is your enemy always
And expects himself to rule   over this Roman empire   520
Which all his ancestors owned   save for Uther alone.

 'The New Year's notice you sent,   I made known by myself
Before that named noble   and all his nine kings; †
In that most royal palace   of the Round Table
I summonsed him solemnly,   as seen by his knights;   525
In faith, never in my life   was I ever more fearful,
And many a princely palace   have I passed through on earth!
I would shed all my staff   and my standing in Rome
Before serving that Sovereign   with another such message!
He was made chosen chieftain,   chief of all others,   530
For his achievements in arms,   his unmatched charming chivalry;
For his wisdom and worthiness,   and the weight of his power.
Of all those which I know of,   in this whole world,
He is created most knightly   of all across Christendom
Of any conqueror or king   that is crowned on earth;   535
Of countenance, of courage   and of cutting expression,
He is the most comely knight   active now under Christ!
He is spoken as one   who despises silver,
A man who regards gold   no more than great stones,
Nor rates wine more than water   that runs in his wells;   540
Nor wants for worldly wealth   save the renown of honour. †
In no rich country abroad   was known such comport and courtesy
As shown by this Conqueror   and beheld by his court;
At Christmas I counted,   of kings all anointed,
With him, wholly ten,   at his table that time.   545

46

He will make war, I think,   so I urge you beware;
Pay well many warriors   and watch all your borders
And be ready arrayed   to respond at the quickest,
For if he reaches Rome,   the ransom will be endless. †
I deem it wise you get ready   and delay no longer;   550
Be sure of your paid soldiers,   send them to the mountains, †
For in quite just three months,   if he stays quick and hale,
He will with great power   hasten here on his way!'

'By Easter,' says the Emperor,   'my own end is thus:
To be armed across Germany   with my knights arrayed;   555
And fare firmly to France,   that flower of all realms,
So to fetch that fellow   and forfeit his lands.
     For I shall set captains   both cunning and noble,
And great men of Genoa,   giants at jousting,
To meet him in the mountains   and martyr his knights,   560
Strike them strong in the valleys   and destroy them for ever!
We shall raise a great watchtower   up there upon Gotthard,
To be garrisoned and guarded   with good men at arms,
With a beacon above   to burn when they like,
So no enemy host   shall enter the mountains.   565
On Mount Bernard   there shall be built another,
Bustling with bannerets   and noble bachelors,
And no prince shall pass   through the gates of Pavia,
Because my prized knights   shall make that place perilous!'

Then lordly Sir Lucius   sends several letters,   570
All bound for the Orient,   by his most austere knights;
To Ambyganye and Orcage,   Alexandria also, †
To India and Armenia,   riding by the Euphrates,
     To Asia and Africa   and far beyond Europe,
To where they speak Elamite   and out still to Hyrcania, †   575
To Arabia and Egypt   in search of those lords
That each holds their land by decree,   in those eastern marches
Of Damascus and Damietta,   as dukes and earls.
They addressed themselves quickly   for dread of his dislike;
Honourable kings   from Crete and Cappadocia   580
Came at his command   directly at once;

To Tartary and Turkey,   after they receive tidings,
Come terrible tyrants,   turning by Thebes,
And the flower of that fair folk   of Amazon lands;
All shall forfeit their realms   who fail to take the field!   585
From Babylon and Baghdad   the noblest knights,
Boys and high barons   bide idling no longer;
From Persia, Pamphilia   and the lands of Prester John,
Each prince with all power   prepared in full view;
The Sultan of Syria   assembles his knights   590
From the Nile to Nazareth   in mighty numbers;
From Gadara to Galilee   there gathered at once
The most trusted Sultans   and servants to Rome;
On the Greek Sea they gathered,   with grievous weapons,
In their great galleys   with glittering shields;   595
On the sea for the Sultan   waits the Cypriot king,
With all the royalty of Rhodes   arrayed with him alone;
They sailed with a stiff wind   over salt swells,
Swiftly, those Saracens,   as they saw fit.
At Corneto with craft   the kings all alight   600
With the city of Rome   just sixty miles hence.
The Greeks likewise were gathered   in a great number;
The mightiest of Macedonia,   and men from those marches
Of Apulia and Prussia,   pressing on with others,
Like the liegemen of Lithuania   in endless legions.   605
And thus in countless sums   did those soldiers form up,
Sultans and Saracens   from sundry lands
And the Sultan of Syria,   with sixteen kings;
All assembled at once   at the city of Rome.

 Then out comes the Emperor,   armed all entirely,   610
Arrayed with his Romans   riding stout steeds;
Sixty giants before them,   engendered by fiends,
With witches and warlocks   to watch on his tents,
Anywhere that he wends,   wintertime or whenever.
Too heavy for horses,   those heartless churls   615
Ride on covered camels,   mail-clad and in towers; [†]
He advances with his aliens,   arrayed in a huge host,
And into all Germany,   by right owned by Arthur,

Rides in by the river   with reckless abandon,
And raids with a free will   across all those high lands;   620
Westphalia, by warfare,   he wins as he likes,
And draws in by the Danube   and dubs his new knights;
He besieges great castles   in the country of Cologne
And sojourns all that season   with countless Saracens.

At the Octaves of Hilary,   Sir Arthur himself [†]   625
Commands all his lords   in his much-acclaimed council:
'Decamp to your countries,   collect all of your knights,
Then come to Cotentin   completely arrayed
And bide for me at Barfleur,   on blissful waves,
With the best of your men   all boldly aboard;   630
And I will meet you most royally   in those fair marches!'
Suddenly, he sends forth   sergeants at arms
To all his mariners in order   to commandeer ships;
Within sixteen days   his fleet was assembled
On the salt sea at Sandwich,   to set sail when ready.   635
He holds a parliament   in the palace of York, [†]
With all his peers of the realm,   prelates and others;
And after their prayers,   in the presence of his lords,
The king speaks these words,   as he thought best counsel:
'It is my purpose to pass   upon perilous ways,   640
To strike out with my keen men   and conquer those lands,
And outrage my enemy,   if fortune may prevail,
That occupies my inheritance,   the Empire of Rome.
I assign here a sovereign,   for your kind assent,
The son of my dear sister;   Sir Mordred himself [†]   645
Shall be my lieutenant   with allotted authority
Over all those loyal liegemen   who hold my lands.'
Then he speaks to his kinsman,   in that council himself;
'I make you keeper, Sir Knight,   of many great kingdoms,
A worshipful warden   to rule my wards and lands   650
That I have won by war   in all this wide world.
I want Guinevere, my wife,   to be held in renown
And that she wants for naught,   she must have what she wishes;
See that my choicest castles   are completely equipped
So that she may sojourn there   in seemly estate;   655

See my forests are fenced,   kept friendly for ever,
That none may hunt my game   save for Guinevere,
And that in the season   when grease is assigned,
She takes what she pleases   when the time is so right. †
Chancellor and Chamberlain,   change them as you will,   660
Auditors and officers,   ordain them yourself;
So too juries and judges,   my judiciary here,
Dealing justice to those   who would work only injury.
If I am destined to die   by the dear will of God,
I choose you as executor,   chief in charge of my will,   665
To administer my goods   – so my soul is made restful –
To mendicants and those   caught by misery or mischief.
Take here my testament   of my great treasure;
I leave this in your trust,   so do not ever betray me
Or you will answer before   that most austere Judge   670
Who directs all this world   as He wishes and deems;
So look that my last will   is carried out loyally!
You have complete care   of what my crown asserts,
Of all my worldly wealth   and of my wife too;
See that you keep so clean   that there be no complaints   675
When I come back to this country,   if Christ will allow it.
If you have the good grace   to govern with wisdom,
I will crown you, kinsman knight,   as a king with my hands.' †

Then Sir Mordred, most mildly,   opening his mouth,
Kneeled to the Conqueror   and speaks these words calmly: 680
'I loyally beseech you,   as my blood lord,
That you should for charity   choose yourself another,
     For if you put me in this plight,   you deceive your people;
To present myself as princely   is but a simple power;
And while those who work war   are worshipped thereafter,   685
I will, set against them,   have but little esteem.
To campaign in your presence   is what I prefer;
My provisions are packed   and my prized knights are ready!' †

'You are my nearest nephew,   my nursling of old,
That I have chided and cheered,   a child of my chamber;   690
For your shared blood with me,   do not forsake this office;

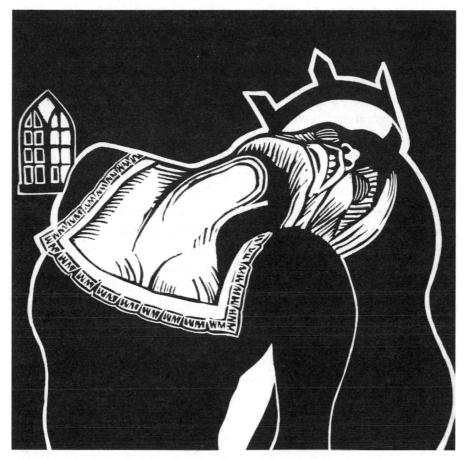

And his wife suddenly sighs   when he asked for his sword
And sways in a swoon   just as if she were dying!

You know what it means   if you will not do my bidding!'
Now he takes his leave   and lingers no longer
With those lords and liegemen   whom he leaves behind;
And then that worthy one   went into his chamber   695
    So to comfort his queen   in her melancholy.
Weeping, Guinevere   kisses him weakly
And talks to him tenderly   with many tears:
'How I curse that one   who did cause this war,
And takes my wedded lord,   and his worship, away;   700
All that I love in life   thus wends from this land
And I believe I am left   forever lost and alone!

My dear lord I would rather   die here in your arms
Than endure in despair   this dread fate alone!'
'Grieve not, Guinevere,   for all God's love in heaven;   705
Do not grudge me my going,   it shall turn to good!
Your sorrow and weeping   straight wounds my heart;
For all the wealth in the world,   I wish I this woe was not here;
I leave you with a keeper,   a knight you can call your own,
As overlord of England   under yourself,   710
And that is Sir Mordred   whom you have much praised,
Who will do your bidding,   my dear, as you order.'
Then he takes his leave   from that room and those ladies,
Kissed them most kindly   and entrusts them to Christ;
And his wife suddenly sighs   when he asked for his sword   715
And sways in a swoon   just as if she were dying!
He pressed to his palfrey   in the presence of his lords,
Spurs from the palace   with his prized knights,
That right royal company   of the Round Table,
And sped towards Sandwich;   she sees him no more.   720

There the great ones were gathered   with their gleeful knights,
Gracing the green field   and grandly arrayed;
Leading dukes and high lords   ride with great display,
Earls of all England   with archers enough. †
The sheriffs then sharply   shift soldiers about,   725
Arrange them before   all that rich Round Table,
And assign those from each country   command of certain lords,
In the south, on that seashore,   to sail when ready.
Then barges were unbound   and rowed to the bank,
And horses brought on board   with noble helms   730
And trussed up tightly,   those mounts with their trappings;
Then tents and catapults   and toughened shields,
Camp cabins and clothes bags   and noble coffers,
Rough hacks and hackneys   and horses for war; †
Thus they stow all the stuff   for these sternest of knights. †   735

With all ships ready as should be,   they shunned further delay
And untied them promptly   as the tide turns;
Cogs and crayers   then cross their masts
On command of the king,   unfurling sails quickly;

They weigh those great anchors   with graft at the wale,   740
Did those watermen wise   to the power of the waves.
Then folk at the forecastles   coil the ropes fully
Of flat barges, freight ships   and Flemish vessels,
Tighten sails at the tops   to trim out the luffs,
Then stand at the starboard   and sing stout and bold.   745
The prized ships of that port   prove and test their draught,
Then fare at full sail   over the foaming waves;
They haul in their boats   wholly without any harm
And shipmen sharply   then shutter portholes, †
Launch leads upon luffing   to sound all the depths, †   750
Look to the lodestar   when the light fails,
And set course by craft,   when the cloud lifts,
With the needle and stone   on the night tides. †
For dread of the dark night,   they slowed down a little
And the sailors in that stream   all struck sail at once.   755

The king was in a great cog,   with a crowd of his knights,
Enclosed in his cabin   in courtly array;
Within, on a rich bed,   he rests a little,
And with the swell of the sea,   he slipped into dreams.
He dreamed of a dragon,   dreadful to behold,   760
Driving over the deep   to drown all his people,
Come sweeping quickly   out of the west lands,
Unworthily wandering   over the wild waves;
Both his head and his neck   were wholly all over
Glazed as of blue,   enamelled full fair;   765
His shoulders were scaled   all like clear silver
Like shields, on that shrimp,   with shrinking points;
His womb and his wings,   of wonderful hues,
Were like marvellous mail   all mounted on high;
His tail was toothed   with a great many tongues   769 (a)
Whoever so touched it   was lost for ever!   770
His feet were furnished   all in fine sable
And his claws were encased   with clearest gold;   771 (b)
And such a venomous flare   flew from his lips
That the flowing sea flood   seemed to be all on fire!

Then out of the Orient   came forth against him
A black bustling bear   above in the clouds,   775
With each paw as on posts,   with massive palms
And with perilous claws   swept and curved in appearance;
Repellent and loathsome   were his locks and his looks,
With his legs all bowed,   lopsided and horrible,
Fur tangled and filthy   and, with his foaming lips,   780
Was the foulest of figures   that ever was formed!
He bounded and bellowed   and thereafter brandished
His brutal claws   all bustling for battle;
He so reared up and roared   that he rocked all the earth;
So rudely he rapped   he angered even himself!   785

Then from deep in the distance   came that dragon against him
And with drubbing he drove him   abroad all the welkin;
He fares like a falcon,   and freely he strikes;
Both with feet and with fire   he fights all at once.
The bear in that battle though,   he seemed the bigger,   790
And bites his foe boldly   with baleful teeth;
Such blows he delivers   with his broad claws,
That his breast and his belly   were bloody all over.
He ripped and he raked   like to rive all the world,
Such that running red blood   falls like rain from the heavens! 795
He would have wearied that worm   by the weight of his power
Were it not for the wild fire   that it spewed in defence.

Then that worm wanders up   away upon high
And comes gliding down   striking hard from the clouds,
Attacks him with his talons   and tears at his spine –   800
Between tail and top   over ten feet long! –
Then he butchered that bear   and blew out his life,
And let him fall to the foam   so to float where he would.
This bad dream so troubled   that bold ship-bound king
That his brain near bursts for woe   on the bed where he lies. 805

Then that wise king wakens   all weary from troubling
And talks with two scholars,   both constant companions,
Taught in the seven sciences,   with most subtle skills, †

'A dragon and dread bear   so disturbed my slumber
That they made me most weary;   please explain my dream'

Well-schooled and cultured,   the best under Christ;
He told them of his torment   in his tortured sleep: 810
'A dragon and dread bear   so disturbed my slumber
That they made me most weary;   please explain my dream
Lest I swift swoon and die,   as God might so wish!'

'Sir,' they said quickly,   these scholars most wise,
'The dragon you dreamed of,   so dreadful a sight,   815
That drove over the deep   to drown all your people,

55

Surely and certainly,   it is yourself
Who sails over the sea   with your steadfast knights:
The colours so cast   upon his clear wings
We think are those of your kingdoms   that you have rightly won.   820
And that many-toothed tail   with its huge tongues?
It betokens your fair folk   who travel with your fleet.
The bear that was beaten   above in the clouds
Betokens the tyrants   who torment your people
Or else some giant   that would seek to engage you   825
In single combat   with yourself alone;
And you shall have victory,   with the help of Our Lord,
As you in your vision   were so clearly shown.
Be you daunted no more   by this dreadful dream
Nor concerned, Sir Conqueror,   but comfort yourself   830
And those who sail the seas   with your steadfast knights.'

With trumpets blown tightly,   they trim their sails
And at once this array   rows right over the sea;
Now they quickly come   to the Normandy coast;
Blithely at Barfleur,   those nobles alighted   835
And find a fleet there already   with many of their friends;
The flower of the fairest folk   of fifteen realms.
These kings and captains   had kept faith with their vow
As that king had commanded   at Carlisle that Christmas.

Yet, when they set foot on land   and pitched their tents,   840
There turns up a Templar   who told the king swiftly: .
'There is a tyrant near here   who torments your people,
A great giant of Genoa,   engendered by fiends;
He has forced down his throat   more than five hundred folk
And uncountable infants   from high-born families.   845
This has been his sustenance   these last seven winters
But it saddens him not   for he likes it so much!
No clan exists   in the country round Cotentin –
Lest it keeps a castle   with strong curtain walls –
Which has come to escape   the cruel death of its sons, †   850
Who he carried to his crag   and then cleanly devoured!
The duchess of Brittany   has been taken today,

56

As she rode beside Rennes   with her retinue of knights;
He led her to the mountain,   where that devil longs
To lie with that lady   while she still remains living.   855
We followed her from afar,   more than five hundred
Barons and burghers   and noble bachelors,
But he climbed to his crag;   she cried screaming so loud
On account of that creature   it will come ever to haunt me!
She was the flower of all France,   and across the five realms †   860
Was one of the fairest   in form ever born;
The gentlest of jewels,   as adjudged by great lords,
From Genoa to Gironne   by Jesus of heaven!
She is kinswoman to your queen,   as you most likely know,
Descended from the richest   that reigns upon earth;   865
As you are rightly our king,   for your people have pity
And pray rise in revenge   for those so rebuked!'

'Alas,' says Sir Arthur,   'in all my long life,
Not to be warned of this   has dimmed my renown!
I am not fairly favoured   and I am foully tarnished   870
To learn that this fiend   has defiled this fair lady!
I would have forfeited   fifteen years of French taxes
To have stood but a furlong   away from that fellow
When he stole that lady   and led her to the mountains;
I would much lose my life   before harm befell her!   875
If you could show me the crag   where that cruel one dwells,
I would climb up that cliff   and speak with him there,
To treat with that tyrant   for his treason here
And make a truce for a time   till things betide better.' †

'Sire, do you see that far headland   with those two fires beyond?   880
You will find that fiend there,   unfettered in his doings,
On the crest of that crag,   by a cold spring,
Which carpets the cliffs   with its cascading waters;
There you will find folk   left flat dead without number,
And more florins, in faith,   than all France could muster,   885
For that traitor has gathered   more treasure by tricks
Than was taken from Troy,   as I know, in past times.'

Then that regal king rages   with regret for those people,
Goes right towards a tent,   but could no longer rest!
He writhes and he wrestles,   he wrings his hands;   890
There was no one in this world   who could know what this meant!
He calls Sir Kay,   his loyal cup-bearer,
And Sir Bedevere the bold,   who bore his great sword:
'Look here, after evensong,   be armed and ready
By those bushes on horseback,   next to those blithe streams,   895
For I will privately pass   on a pilgrimage then, †
At supper time   when all my lords are served,
So to seek a saint,   by those salt streams
On the Mount of Saint Michael,   where miracles are made.'

After evensong,   Sir Arthur himself   900
Went to his wardrobe   and threw off his garments,
And armed himself in his aketon,   adorned with embroidery;
Over that, on the outside,   a jerkin of Acre leather;
Just above it a jazerant   of gentle mail;
Then a jupon of Jerodine   with jagged trimmings;   905
He puts on a bascinet   burnished bright as of silver,
The best made in Basel,   bordered most richly; †
The crest and the circlet   decorated that helm
Clasped in clear gold   graced with clusters of stones;
The visor, the aventail,   were of such fine work   910
As to be void of defect,   with windings of silver; †
His gloves were gilt gaily   and engraved at the hems
With gadlings on those gauntlets   of glorious hews;
He belts on a broad shield   and asks for his blade;
Then he bounds to a brown steed   and bides there before   915
He steps into a stirrup   and swings aloft,
And straightens up stoutly,   stirring most boldly,
Then spurs that bay steed   and rides abrupt to the bushes
Where his keen knights waited,   complete like for war. †

Then they rode by that river   which ran so swiftly;   920
There, regal boughs   overhung from great trees;
The roe and the reindeer   ran freely there †
In brushwood and roses   to revel in pleasure:

The forests all flourished   with a full many flowers,
And falcons and pheasants   of fabulous hues;   925
Every fowl flaps about here   that can fly with wings
And there sang the great cuckoo   all loud from the groves;
With boundless glad rapture   they gladden themselves:
Sweet were the notes   as sung by the nightingale
That threaped with the thrushes –   three hundred at once!   930
That swift splashing of water   and singing of birds
Might assuage the worst sorrow   of he whose life was the
      saddest! †

Then these folk fare   and alight now on foot,
Fastening their fair steeds   some few feet away;
And then keenly that king   commanded his knights   935
To bide by their horses   and to be stood there;
'For I will seek this saint   by myself alone
And talk with this main man   who claims this mount,
And afterwards either of you   can make offerings accordingly
With esteem to Saint Michael,   who sits mighty with Christ!'   940

The king comes to the crag   with its soaring cloughs,
And he climbs aloft   to the crest of the cliff,
Casts up his visor   and he looks keenly,
Catching some cold air   to comfort himself.
Two fires he finds,   flaming full high;   945
He fares between them   a fourth of a furlong;
He wandered at once   the way by the well-springs
To know of that warlock   and where he dwells.
He goes forth to the first fire   and then he finds
A widow most woeful,   wringing her hands,   950
And grieving by a grave,   with gushing tears,
That was new made since mid-day,   judging by the mound.
He spoke to that sad woman   with soothing words
And with feeling, as fitting,   asked after that fiend.

Then this woeful woman   greets him with sorrow,   955
Climbed up from her knees   and clasped her hands,
And said, 'Be careful, kind sir,   you speak far too loud!

If that warlock knows of you,   he will savage us all!
Let that one be well cursed   who stole all of your wits
And made you come this way   among these wild waters!   960
I warn you, by heaven,   your reward will be sorrow!
Why clamber here, noble?   You seem but unblessed!
Do you think you will beat him   with your bright broadsword?
Were you stronger than Wade   or even Gawain †
You will win no renown,   I warn you now!   965
No blessing will save you   from he you seek in these crags;
Not six of you   would have the strength to slay him,
For once your eyes set upon him   you will lose the heart
To cross yourself for safety   on account of his size!

'You are noble and fair   and in your first flower,   970
But you are fated to fall,   which fills me with grief!
Were there fifty such folk   as you in the field,
That fellow with one fist   would fell you all at once.
Behold this dear duchess –   just today she was taken –
Dug deep in and buried,   dead in this ground;   975
He had murdered this mild one   by when mid-day was rung,
Without mortal mercy –   to me it seemed meaningless;
He defiled her by force   and left her frozen dead;
He slayed her with savagery   and slit her to the navel.
So I have embalmed her   and buried her after;   980
Her bearing so troubled me   I shall never see bliss!
Yet for all of her friends   not one followed after
But me, her foster-mother   of full fifteen years!
I shall never fare forth   from this foreland again
And shall be found in this field   till the day I fall dead.' 985

Then Sir Arthur answers   to that old wife,
'I have come from the Conqueror,   courteous and noble,
As one of the best   of those knights of King Arthur
And messenger to this mire   to amend matters
By speaking with this monster   who masters this mount;   990
I will treat with this tyrant   by offering him treasure
And make a truce for a time   until things are better.'

'Yah! Your words are but waste,' said that wife then,
'For he holds little regard for land, leases or people;
And neither rents nor red gold does he care about   995
For he acts as he likes and lives outside the law
Without licence of lordship, to rule as he will. †
He is cloaked in a kirtle which he keeps for himself
That was spun in Spain, by special ladies,
And sewn together in Greece with the greatest of skill;   1000
It resembles a whole hide of hair all over,
All bordered with the beards of the noblest of kings,
All curled and combed so that knights will recognise
Each king by his colour and from what country he hails.
Here he fleeces the funds from fifteen realms;   1005
For each Easter Eve, whenever that falls,
They send him their receipts for the sake of their people,
Safely that season with selected knights.
All these seven years he has sought Arthur's beard;
Therefore he lives up here to horrify his people   1010
Until the British king has burnished his lips by shaving
And sent his beard to this beast with his best nobles.
If you have brought no beard, please abandon your quest,
For you will bear boundless grief if you bring him aught else;
For he has more treasure to take when he wants   1015
Than was ever Arthur accorded or any of his elders.
Yet if you do bring the beard, he will be more blissful
Than if you gave him Burgundy or the whole of Great Britain;
But look now, for charity, please chastise your lips
So that no words escape whatsoever betides.   1020
Let your present be prepared, but do not pester him,
For he is at his supper and is soon annoyed.
Pray, heed my clear counsel and take off your armour,
Kneel compliant in your kirtle and call him your lord.
He dines all this season on seven young sons,   1025
Chopped up in a charger of chalk-white silver,
With pickles and powders made from precious spices,
And syrup-sweet wine most plenteous from Portugal;
His braising spits turned by three abject damsels,
They then bide at his bedtime to do all his bidding;   1030

61

And four more should fall dead   within just four hours
Lest his lust be fulfilled   that his foul flesh yearns for.'

'Ha! I have brought that beard,'   he says, 'which suits me better;
I bear it on my body   so I will clamber on,
But, lady, pray tell me   where that foul one lives?   1035
Shall Our Lord let me live   I shall laud you always!'

'Fare fast to that fire,' she said,   'that flares up so high;
There, that fiend feeds himself;   test him as you feel.
But you must pass by the side,   somewhat to the south,
For he can sniff out your scent   more than six miles away.'   1040

He then set out swiftly   to the source of that smoke,
Signed himself with the cross,   with some words for safety,
And passed unseen by that savage   till he reached the site;
How unseemly he sat,   that sot supping alone!
He lay languid and long,   lodging most foul,   1045
The thigh of a man's limb   he lifts up by the haunch;
His back and his buttocks,   and his broad loins,
He bakes by that bonfire,   seemingly without breeches;
There were roasts full rude,   and rueful turned flesh
Of boys and beasts   both braised on a spit,   1050
And a cauldron crammed full   with christened children,
Some braised like brisket   spun on spits by maidens.

Then this comely king,   on account of his people,
His troubled heart bleeds   where he stands on the boulders;
Then he shouldered his shield,   shirking no longer,   1055
Brandishes his broadsword   by its bright hilt,
Rushes on that ruffian   right with a raged will
And hails highly that hulk   with these haughty words:

'Now, all-wielding God,   who all of us worship,
Give you sorrow, sir,   and distress where you lie   1060
For you are the filthiest fellow   that ever was formed!
How foully you feed,   may the Fiend have your soul!
Here is cookery unclean,   cur, I do swear,

That glutton was aghast   and glowered all ugly

You crud of all creatures,   you cursed wretch!
Because you have killed   all these christened children,   1065
Making martyrs of them,   by murderous ways,
That are here burned and basted,   broken by your hands,
I shall mete out such payment   as you have much earned
Through the might of Saint Michael   to whom this mount belongs.
And for this fair lady   who you left to die,   1070
And forced on the field   for your own filthy ends,
Get you ready, dog-son,   let the Devil have your soul,
For you shall die this day   by dint of my hand!'

That glutton was aghast   and glowered all ugly;
He grinned like a greyhound   with grisly teeth;   1075
He gaped and groaned fast   with grudging looks
For grief at that good king   who greets him with anger!
His foul hair and forelocks   were formless and matted
And out of his mouth   frothed foam half a foot;
All his face and his forehead   resembled all over   1080
The fell of a frog,   and seemed to be freckled;
He was hook-nosed like a hawk,   with a hoary beard
And hairy whole to his eyes,   with hanging brows;
Harsh as a hound-fish,   if you looked hard enough,
Was the hide of that hulk,   wholly all over!   1085
He had huge great ears,   all ugly to show,
With fully horrible eyes,   surely aflame;
Flat-mouthed like a flounder,   with sneering lips flaring,
And the flesh of his front fangs   was foul like a bear;
His beard, bold and black,   reached down to his breast   1090
All swollen like a porpoise   with a massive carcase,
And all flapped the flesh   in his foul lips,
That wreathed like a wolf   all snarling with wrath!
Bull-necked was that beast,   and broad in the shoulders,
Its breast blotched like a boar   with enormous bristles,   1095
Rough arms like an oak tree   with wrinkled bark,
In limb and loin loathsome,   that you can believe;
Shovel-footed was that savage,   sheathed surely in scales,
With shapeless shanks   shoved together at the knees;
Thick thighs like a Goliath,   and thicker in the haunch,   1100
Grown gross like a pig,   most grisly he looks!
Why, the length of that fellow,   it could truly be said,
Was from face to foot   over five fathoms tall.

Then up he starts sturdily   on his two stout shanks,
And quickly catches his club   made all of clean iron!   1105
He would have killed the king   with this cruel weapon
But, by the craft of Christ,   this monstrous cur failed
Though the crest and the circlet,   and its clasps of silver,
He struck clean with his club,   that came crashing down!

The king casts up his shield   and protects himself,   1110
And with his bold broadsword   deals him a great blow;
He hits his great foe   full straight in the face
So that burnished blade   runs straight to the brain;
He wiped his forehead fully   with his foul hands
And fast and fiercely thereafter   hits the face of Arthur!   1115
The king changes foot,   a little askew;
Had that chop chanced to hit him,   evil would be achieved;
He follows up fiercely   and fastens such a blow,
High up on the haunch   with his hard weapon,
That he buried his sword   half a foot deep,   1120
So the hot blood of that hulk   runs down to the hilt;
He strikes right at that giant,   gouging into his guts
Just down to the genitals,   and jagged them asunder!
Then he raged and roared   and angrily strikes
Full eagerly at Arthur   but fails, hitting earth;   1125
His swing swipes the sward   by the length of a sword,
And that king nearly swoons   with the sweep of his blows!
Yet from these swishes   the king swiftly swings back,
And swipes in with his sword   so it swirled through the loins;
Both the guts and the gore   gush out all at once,   1130
So that all gleams the grass   on the ground where he stands!
Then he casts down his club   and he seizes the king;
He caught him in his arms   on the crest of the crag
And clamps him completely   to crush his ribs;
He holds that king so hard   that his heart nearly bursts!   1135
Then those abject maidens   tumble bitterly to earth,
Kneeling and crying   and said, clasping their hands:
'Christ, care for that knight   and keep him from sorrow
And do not let that fiend   steal his life from him!'

Yet still that wild warlock   rolls with the king;   1140
They writhe with great wrath   and wrestle together,
And welter and wallow   through those wild bushes,
Quick tumbling and turning,   they tear all their clothes,
From the top in a tussle   they tumble together;
Arthur at once is above,   while sometimes now the other,   1145
From the height of the hill   down to the hard rock,

Fighting on without fail   by the foam on the shore;
But then, with an anelace,   Arthur stabs with ardour,
And hits that hulk often   right up to the hilt.
That thief in his death-throes   squeezed so thoroughly   1150
That he thrust asunder   three ribs of King Arthur!

Then Sir Kay so keenly   leaps towards the king
And said, 'Alas we are lost!   My lord is confounded,
Overthrown by a fiend –   ours is foul fortune!
By faith, we are finished,   forced never to return!'   1155
Then they heave up his hauberk   to handle his body,
Feel his hide and his haunches,   then higher to his shoulders,
His flanks and his fillets   and his fair thighs
And both his back and his breast   and his brawny arms.
They were thankful to find   no injured flesh   1160
And these most gentle knights   judged this outcome most joyous.

'Now surely,' says Sir Bedevere,   'it seems, by my Lord,
He who seldom seeks saints   the more surely he grips them
That clutches this corpse   that came from these high cliffs,
And clasps such a creature   as close to him as silver!   1165
Yet such a martyr, by Michael,   I have much doubt
That our Sovereign Lord   would suffer him in heaven!
And if all saints are as such   that do serve Our Lord,
I shall never no saint be,   by the soul of my father!'

Then with blithe banter   the bold king answers Bedevere: 1170
'Such a saint have I sought,   so help me our Lord!
Therefore bring out your broadsword,   run its blade through his
     heart;
Be sure of this, sir,   he has sorely grieved me!
I have not fought such a fellow   these past fifteen winters –
Save in the mountains of Araby   where I met such another – †   1175
He was more forceful by far   than near any I have found;
Had not fortune been fair,   then I would have been felled!
So now strike off his head   and stake it thereafter;
Give it to your squire,   for he is well horsed,
And bear it to Sir Howell   who is haunted by sorrow   1180

And bid him hearten well   for his foe is destroyed!
Then bear it to Barfleur   and bind it in iron
And set it on the barbican   to show all the nobles.
My blade and my broad shield   still lie on the boulders
On the crest of that crag   where we first encountered,   1185
And nearby that club   made all of clean iron
That has killed many Christians   in these Cotentin lands;
Fly to that foreland   and fetch me that weapon
And let us fare to our fleet   on the foam where it waits.
If you want of his treasure,   take what you like;   1190
I have his kirtle and club   so I covet naught else!'

Now these comely knights   then climb to that crag
And brought him his broad shield   and his bright sword,
The club and coat also,   carried by Sir Kay,
And with the Conqueror they carry them   to show all the kings   1195
What the king had concealed   and had kept for himself
While clear day from the clouds   had climbed upon high.

With that, a great clamour   came to the court,
And before that comely king,   they knelt and cried at once:
'Welcome, our liege lord,   you have dwelled too long!   1200
Governor below God,   most great and noble,
To whom grace is granted   and given at His will,
Now your comely coming   has brought us all comfort!
You have in your royalty   revenged all your people!
Through the help of your hand,   your foes are overthrown   1205
Who ran rough with your folk,   robbing them of their children;
Was there never such relief   for a realm thus so ravaged!'

Then with Christian words   that Conqueror speaks to them all:
'I thank God for His grace,' he said,   'no one else is so great,
For this was no deed of man   but the might of Himself   1210
Or a miracle of His Mother   who is most mild of all.' †
Then sharply he summoned   the sailors thereafter
To shift with the shire-men   and share out all the goods:
'Give all that great treasure   this traitor had stolen
To commoners, clergy   and others of this country;   1215

See that it be done   and dealt to my dear people
That none complains on their part,   on pain of your lives.'
He commands his cousin   with courteous words,
To make a church on that crag   where lay the corpse of that
    lady,
And a convent too made   in homage of Christ,   1220
In memory of that martyr   who lies on the mountain.

When Sir Arthur the King   had killed that giant,
Then blithely that morning   he bustles from Barfleur,
With his battle all broad   spread on those blithe streams;
Towards Castle Blank   he chooses his path,†   1225
    Through a cheerful plain   and under chalk hills;
The king looks for a ford   by the fresh-flowing strand
And fares with his fair folk   over this at his leisure;
That stout one steps forth   and strikes his tents
Strongly set by a stream,   safe on those strait lands.   1230

And so after mid-day,   during mealtime,
Two messengers come   from those far marches
Of the Marshal of France,   greeting him with much honour,
Seeking succour of him   and saying these words:
'Sir, your Marshal and minister   with true mercy prays   1235
That your mighty majesty   shall mete out revenge
For your marcher men   that have suffered mischance
And are harmed beyond measure   in spite of their arms.
I come to inform you   the Emperor has entered France
With a huge and horrible   host of your enemies;   1240
He burns all of Burgundy   with its wealthy boroughs
And beats your nobility   who inhabit those lands;
He keenly encroaches,   by his skill at arms,
Countries and castles   which belong to your crown,
Confounding your commoners,   clergy and others;   1245
Sir King, lest you come,   they shall never recover!
He fells several forests,   forays into your lands,
Spares no fellow their freedom   but affrights your people;
Thus he fells your folk   and pilfers their goods;
Truly, the French tongue   is finished by foreigners!†   1250

He draws into dear France,   as Germans describe,
Dressed with his dragons,   dreadful to see;
By dint of their swords   they do all to death,
Dukes and great leaders,   who dwell therein;
So these landed lords,   ladies and others,   1255
Pray, by the love of Peter,   the apostle of Rome,
That you present at a place   where you will proffer battle
To that unpleasant prince   in due process of time.
He fairs in yonder hills,   beneath those high holts,
And holds there with his great host   of heathen kings;   1260
Help us now for His love   who sits in high heaven
And dauntless talk to them   that would topple us!'

The king bids Sir Boice: 'Bustle up brightly!
Take Sir Berill with you   and Bedevere the rich,
Sir Gawain and Sir Gerin,   these gallant knights,   1265
And gallop to those green woods,   giving this my message:
Say to Sir Lucius   that he works most ignobly,
Foully and lawlessly   troubling my people;
If I am granted life,   I will halt him quickly,
Or many will lose their lives   that follow him on land;   1270
Thus command him keenly   with these cold words
To clear out of my kingdom   with his cruel knights;
If in case he will not,   that accursed wretch,
He can come here for the courtesy   of single combat;
Then we will reckon right quickly   by what right he claims   1275
Thus to ransack this realm   and ravage its people!
There shall it dearly be dealt   with death blows done by hand
What God at Doomsday   shall deal as he likes!'

Now these gallant knights   gather to go
All glittering and golden   upon their great steeds,   1280
Towards the green wood,   with their ground weapons,
To greet well that great lord   who would meet his grief soon.

Then by a wood, on a hill,   these high knights halted
And beheld that great host   of high-held heathen kings;
They heard from their hiding place   a full many hundreds   1285

69

Of elephant horns   all blown full highly;
Pavilions were pitched proudly,   all richly draped
In palls of purple   with precious stones;
And pennons and pennants   with the arms of rich princes
Were placed on that meadow   in plain sight of all people.   1290
Thus, the Romans so richly   had arrayed all their tents
In a row by the river,   under round hills;
Eminent, in the midst,   is the tent of the Emperor,
With eagles all over   emblazoned most fair;
They saw him and the Sultan   and many senators   1295
Proceed to a vast tent   with sixteen kings
Slipping softly in,   sweetly by themselves,
To dine with that sovereign   on splendid rare meats.
Now they wend over the water,   these worshipful knights,
Through the wood to the dwelling   where those kings were;   1300
Just as they had washed   and wandered to their tables,
Worthy Sir Gawain   speaks with unwelcome words:
'May the might and the majesty   of He who all men honour,
That was made and formed   through the might of Himself,
Bring suffering to your seat,   to the Sultan and others,   1305
Who assemble in this hall;   may sorrow become you!
He who calls himself Emperor   is but a base heretic
Who occupies in error   the Empire of Rome,
Owned in heritage by Arthur,   our honourable king,
Accorded to his ancestors,   save for Uther alone;   1310
May the same dreaded curse   which Cain caught for his brother,
Cling to you, cuckoo,   sitting here with that crown; †
The most ignoble lord   that I ever looked on!
My lord marvels much,   man, I say in truth,
Why you murder his men   who deserve no such misery,   1315
The commoners of his country,   its clergy and others,
That cannot have earned this   and can know naught of arms;
Therefore my comely king,   most courteous and noble,
Commands that you quickly   clear out of his lands
Or come alone, out of knighthood,   to contest him in combat;   1320
Since you covet his crown,   now declare your intent!
My duty is discharged,   challenge me who so will,
Before all your charming chivalry,   chieftains and others.

'Now for certain,' says Sir Gawain,   'much wonder I have
That such an old fool like you   would dare speak such words!'

Pray answer us sharply,   without further shirking,
So we may shift shortly   and show my lord what you will.'   1325

The Emperor answered   with austere words:
'You are from my enemy,   Sir Arthur himself;
Yet it brings naught of honour   to offend one of his knights,
Though you be heated men   and needs must do his deeds.
So say this to your sovereign;   I send him these words,   1330

Were it not for the refinement adhering to my rich table,
You would rapidly repent all your many rude words!
Such a rascal as you here rebukes many lords
All arrayed with their retinues, most regal and noble!
Here I will stay for as long as I wish,   1335
Then saunter to the Seine, to do as I so please,
And besiege all those cities by its salty strands,
Then ride on by the Rhône that runs most fair,
And then hurl down the walls of all his rich castles;
I will not leave in Paris, by due process of time,   1340
His part of any hay pile – he can prove this at leisure!' †

'Now for certain,' says Sir Gawain, 'much wonder I have
That such an old fool like you would dare speak such words!
I would give of all France, the most revered of realms,
Just to fight with you faithfully alone in the field!'   1345
Then Sir Gayous answers with arrogant gall –
Being uncle to the Emperor and himself an earl –
'These Britons were always just braggarts of old!
Lo! How he blurts for all his bright clothes,
That he might bludgeon us all with his bright spangled sword! 1350
Ha! He just barks to boast that boy who stands there!'

Sir Gawain was most grieved at these arrogant words
And goes to that knight with a great growling heart;
With his steely sword he strikes off his head,
Then steps on to his steed and leaves with his stout men! 1355
Then these worshipful knights wend quick through the
  watchmen,
Finding wonderfully many each way that they fared;
Over water they went by the strength of their mounts,
Then slowed to rest for a while by the edge of a wood.
Then fiercely on foot followed folk in great numbers, 1360
And Romans arrayed, upon royal steeds,
Chased our chivalrous knights through stretching fields
Till they reached the chief forest on their chalk-white horses.
But a fellow in fine gold, and festooned in sable,
Came forth on a Frisian horse in flashing armour;   1365

72

With his steely sword   he strikes off his head,

A fair-flourished spear   he rests on his fewter
And falls fast on our folk   with frightening cries.

Then Sir Gawain the good,   upon a grey steed,
Grips to him a great spear   and eagerly strikes him
Through the guts, to the gore   he gouges him such   1370
That all the ground steel   glides straight to his heart!
The knight on his great horse   lies gaunt on the ground,
Full grisly and groaning   for grief at his wounds.
Then presses another,   all proudly arrayed
With bearings of purple   all paled with silver,   1375
Boldly on a brown steed   boiling with rage.

He was a pagan from Persia   who pursued him then;
Sir Boice, unabashed,   bears fast against him;
With a bloodthirsty lance   he bores right through him
So both knight and his broad shield   lie burst on the ground!   1380
Then he pulls out the blade   and bounds back to his brothers.

Then Sir Feltemour, a man   so much praised for his might,
Was moved in this manner   and came menacing quickly,
And galloped at Sir Gawain,   angrily to avenge
His grief for Sir Gayous   who lies on the ground.†   1385
Then Sir Gawain was glad   and rides against him;
With Galuth, his great sword,   he strikes eagerly
And that knight on his courser,   he cleaves him cold asunder
Clean down from the crown,   cutting him in two,
And so he kills the knight   with his acclaimed weapon!   1390

Then a rich Roman leader   roared out to his nobles:
'We shall sorely repent   if we ride much farther!
They are bolder than braggarts   who work such sad blows;
Foulness due befell him   who first named them so!'

Then those regal Romans   reversed all their bridles   1395
And returned to their tents   to tell their lords sadly
How Sir Marshall de Mowne   lies dead in the mud,
Justly out-jousted   for his jesting contempt.
But our men are still chased   by yet more charging chivalry –
Some five thousand folk   all upon their fair steeds –   1400
Fast to a forest,   and over foaming waters,
That flowed from a flat lake   some fifty miles off.
There waited in ambush   noble Britons and bannerets,
All the chief chivalry   of the king's chamber;
They see our men being chased,   pitched from their horses,   1405
And their chieftains chopped down   by those who charged
      on them.

So the British all broke out   in ambush at once,
Boldly at the banner,   all knights of Bedevere,
And ravaged those Romans   who ride by the wood,

All those regal ranks   truly loyal to Rome;   1410
They eagerly strike   and fast engage their enemy,
Did those English earls,   and shout 'Arthur!' with earnest;
They pierce many a breast,   through byrnie and bright shield,
Did those boldest of Britons   with their bright swords.
The Romans were overrun   and roughly wounded,   1415
Rounded up like rogues   by riotous knights!
In disarray all those Romans   retreated at once
And ride away in a rout;   for dread it would seem!
A messenger comes   to Peter the Senator †
And said, 'Sir, surely,   your men are surprised!'   1420
So ten thousand men   he assembled at once
And set suddenly about our men   by the salt strands.
Then were Britons abashed   and somewhat aggrieved,
Yet those bold bannerets   and noble bachelors
Break the Roman battle   with the breasts of their steeds;   1425
Sir Boice with his bold men   works bloodshed indeed!
The Romans then rally   and make better array
And all rush on our men   with their rested horses,
They disperse the most regal ranks   of the Round Table,
Overrun their rear guard   and work great sorrow!   1430

Then the Britons on that plain   bear battling no longer
But fled to the forest   and left the field;
Sir Berill is brought down   and Sir Boice is taken,
The best of our bold men   all balefully wounded;
And so our stout soldiers   stop and make a stand,   1435
All stunned by the strokes   of those stern knights,
And lamented their leader,   he who was overwhelmed,
And beseeched God for succour   to send when He would!

Then Sir Idrus comes,   strongly armed in support,
With five hundred men   all upon fair steeds,   1440
And ask fast of our folk   freshly thereafter
If their friends were fallen   who had fought on the field.
Then Sir Gawain says,   'So help me God,
We have been chased today,   chivvied like hares
And routed by Romans   upon their rich steeds,   1445

75

And we lurked in their lee   like trembling wretches!
I could not hence in my life   look my lord in the eye
If we help him so poorly   who has loved us so much!'

Then bravely the Britons   brought spur to steed
And boldly for battle   ride back to the field;   1450
At the fore all the fierce men   ferociously cry,
Forging through the forest,   refreshed and ready.
The Romans then rapidly   arrayed themselves for the fight
In a row on a broad field,   righting their weapons
By that roaring river,   with their ranks in good order;   1455
And retaining with hardship   Sir Boice in arrest.
Now they surged in assault   by the salt strands;
Our assailants strike   with most savage blows,
With lovely lances aloft   they lunge together,
In livery, most lordly,   on leaping steeds.   1460
Gallant men were run through there   with well-ground weapons;
All grisly and gasping   with ghastly expressions.
Great lords of Greece   grieved in much pain,
Yet swiftly with swords   they swung their blows,
Swift swiping down   swarthy knights to their deaths;   1465
Those taking those swoops   swing, swaying to earth;
Swiftly now to the greensward,   many swoon to their death! †
Sir Gawain the gracious,   how grandly he works;
He greets the greatest   with grisly wounds;
With Galuth, he brings down   the most gallant knights;   1470
He strikes so grimly   for grief of that great lord! †
He rides forth royally   and readily thereafter
To where that royal warrior   was held in arrest:
He rives through robust steel,   he rips through their byrnies,
Robs from them that rich man   and rode back to his camp.   1475
Then Peter the Senator   thereafter pursues him,
Through the press of the people   with his prize knights;
In a public display   to recapture that prisoner,
He plunges through the press   with his proudest champions;
Underhand and with wrath,   he strikes at Sir Gawain   1480
And hits him most wrongly   with a weapon of war;
He bursts right asunder   the byrnie on his back!

Yet Sir Boice was brought forth   despite those dark blows wrought.
Then boldly the Britons   all blow their trumpets
And for bliss of Sir Boice,   who was brought out of bondage,   1485
Those knights then did boldly   bear down in battle;
With sword blades of bright steel,   they battered chain mail;
They stab battling steeds   with their steel weapons, †
And with strength struck down all those   who stood against
    them!

Sir Idrus Fitz Ewain   then screams out, 'Arthur!'   1490
And assaults the Senator   with sixteen knights,
The surest of men   that belonged to our side.
Suddenly this small troop   all set to at once,
Forging fast to those foremost,   with flaming swords
And fiercely fight at the front,   all fresh and most eager;   1495
They fell many fellows,   on the far side of that field,
Flat dead on that fair meadow   by the fresh waters.
Then Sir Idrus Fitz Ewain   adventures forth
And strikes forward eagerly,   alone in the fray,
And seeks out the Senator   and seizes his bridle;   1500
With hostility he said   these suitable words:
'Sir, yield yourself quickly,   if you value your life,
For no gift you can give me   can save yourself;
Have no doubt if you dawdle,   or deign to play tricks,
That you will die on this day   by dint of my blows!'   1505
'I consent,' said the Senator,   'so help me Christ.
As long as I am brought   safely straight to your king;
Ransom me reasonably   and I will raise quickly
The reward which you seek   with revenues from Rome.'
Then Sir Idrus answers   with these austere words: 1510
'You shall have such conditions   as the king may confer,
When you come to his company   to be tried at his court;
He may counsel himself   not to keep you confined
But kill you on command   before all his packed knights.'
They led him through the melee   and removed all his mail   1515
And left him with Lionel   and his brother Lowell.

77

Thus below, on the land,   by those lovely strands,
The liegemen of Sir Lucius   are lost for ever!
Peter the Senator   is taken prisoner!
Full many prize knights   of Port Jaffa and Persia   1520
And many people besides   all perished as well;
In the pressure at that ford   they plunged now in piles!
There might men see Romans   all ruefully wounded,
Run down by riders   of the Round Table,
Who put right their byrnies   by that riverbank,   1525
That ran readily all over,   soaked in red blood!
They placed in their rear guard   the most regal Romans
To ransom for red gold   and royal steeds;
Then they readily exchange   and rest their horses,
And those ranks rode at once   right to their rich king.   1530

A knight canters ahead   and quickly tells the king:
'Sire, your messengers come   with merry news from the mountains;
Today they met in combat   with men of the marches,
And mangled in the morass   with marvellous knights!
In good faith we have fought,   by yonder fresh strands,   1535
With the finest of folk   that belong to your foe;
On that field, fifty thousand   fierce men-at-arms
Are all believed fallen   within just a furlong!
We achieved a choice win,   as Our Lord would so choose,
Against those charging knights   who challenged your people!   1540
The chief chancellor of Rome,   a most noble chieftain,
Seeks a charter of peace,   pleading for your charity;
And Peter the Senator   is taken prisoner.
Pagans enough   from Port Jaffa and Persia
Come prompt from that press,   guarded by your prize knights,   1545
To endure for their pains   poverty in your prisons.
I beseech you, sir,   say to us your desire;
Whether you grant their wish   or you will them woe?
You may have for the Senator   sixty horses laden
With silver by Saturday,   certainly paid,   1550
And for the chief chancellor,   that most noble chevalier,
Carts charged with chests   all chock-full with gold.
The rest of the Romans   will be held in arrest,

Until their ransoms from Rome   are all rightly reckoned.
I beseech you, sire,   speak your will to these lords;   1555
Will you send them overseas   or keep them here for yourself? †
Solemnly, all your best men   are believed safe and sound,
Except Sir Ewain Fitz Henry,   who is wounded on one side.'

'Let Christ be thanked,' spoke the king,   'and His kind Mother!
Who kept you safe with His care   and by His holy skill;   1560
With craft God discomforts   whom He so dislikes;
No miscreant can escape   from the squeeze of His grasp;
Destiny or doughtiness   through deeds of arms,
Are all deemed and dealt with   as God so desires!
So I can thank you for coming,   it comforts us all!   1565
Sir knight,' says the Conqueror,   'so Christ help me,
I grant you, for your tidings,   most wealthy Toulouse,
Its tolls and its tithes   from its taverns and others,
The town and its tenements,   its towers so high,
And all that which is temporal,   while my time lasts. †   1570

'But say to the Senator,   I send him these words:
That no silver shall save him   lest Ewain recovers;
I would sooner see him sink   into salty quicksands
Than see my man stay sick   who is most sorely wounded;
I shall separate those lords,   so help me Christ,   1575
And disperse them all singly   to my several realms.
He shall never again   see his lords sat in Rome,
Nor sit at counsel   with his stately brethren,
For this Conqueror considers   that it becomes of no king
To commune with his captives   and make terms over silver.   1580
I would like him to accept   it becomes naught of knighthood
To speak of commerce   when so taken captive;
It is not up to prisoners   to pressure a lord
Nor demand business parity   in the presence of princes.
I command the Constable,   who governs this castle,   1585
That he be well kept   and in close confinement;
He will know my mandate tomorrow,   before mid-day rings,
To which march he must go   to languish in misery.'

They convey their captive,   taken by men-at-arms,
And commit him to the Constable,   as the king bids,   1590
And then to Arthur they go   and tell him with ardour
The answer of the Emperor,   angered by these deeds.
Then King Arthur, the noblest   above others on earth,
Lauded his lords   at his table that evening:
'Over all other things   I must honour on earth   1595
Are those who venture forth   by themselves in my absence!
I shall love them, God help me,   all the while that I live
And give them lavish lands   wherever they like;
None shall lose that plays my game,   if life is granted to me,
Who are lamed for their loyalty   by these pleasant strands.'   1600

But in the clear dawn   the dear king himself
Commanded Sir Cador,   with his dear knights,
Sirs Cleremus and Cleremond,   with keen men-at-arms,
And Sirs Clowdmur and Clegis,   to convey these lords;
Sir Boice and Sir Berill,   with banners displayed,   1605
Sir Baldwin, Sir Brian   and Sir Bedevere the rich,
Sir Reynald and Sir Richard,   children of Sir Roland,
All to ride with the Romans   down roads with their brethren:
'Spur now most promptly   to Paris resplendent
With Peter the prisoner   and his prize knights;   1610
Entrust them to the provost   in the presence of lords,
On the pain and the peril   which appends to them,
That they be watched wisely   and held by wardens
As wards under warranty   by worshipful knights;
Pay men well with wages,   and want for no silver;   1615
I warn that one well;   if he blunders, beware!'

Now the Britons bound forth   as the king bids,
Busy to their battles,   their banners displayed,
Towards Chartres they charge,   these chivalrous knights,
And quickly achieved   in reaching fair Champagne;   1620
For with might had the Emperor   himself ordered that
Sir Utolf and Sir Evander,   two honourable kings,
Earls of the Orient   with knights most austere,
Hailed the bravest of all   that belonged to his host,

Sir Sextynour of Libya   and many senators,   1625
The King of Syria himself,   with plenty of Saracens;
The senator of Sutri   with great sums of soldiers –
Assigned by that court   with assent of his peers –
To trek as if towards Troyes   some treason to work,
To trap by a trick   our travelling knights,   1630
Having perceived that Peter   would be kept in Paris
By the Provost, imprisoned,   to suffer his plight.
Therefore they busied as bound   with banners displayed,
Through scrub and by bushes,   and on great big horses.
They plant themselves in the path,   with power arrayed   1635
To pilfer those prisoners   back from our prize knights.

Then Sir Cador of Cornwall   commands his peers,
Sir Clegis, Sir Cleremus,   Sir Cleremond the noble:
'Behold the Clough of Clime,   with its cliffs so high;
See this country is clear,   for it has hidden corners;   1640
     Scour it now most surely   through scrub and elsewhere,
So no scrub-hidden scoundrel   scorns us later on;
See you scan it such   that we suffer no scrape,
Or those who skulk will then scoff   at our later discomfort.'

Now these hardy knights   hasten to the holts,   1645
To help their own lords   by harkening for horsemen,
Which they find wholly helmed   and mounted on high,
Halted on the highway   by the holt side.
     With knightly courage and countenance,   Sir Clegis himself
Calls to that company   and speaks these words: 1650
'Is there any kaiser or duke,   or acclaimed knight here,
That would show his craft in arms   on account of his king?
We are come from the king   of this royal country
That is called the Conqueror,   crowned so of its earth;
Here is his rich retinue,   all of the Round Table,   1655
Come ready to ride   where so ever he wills.
We seek warlike jousting,   if you will be so bold,
With the jewels of your knighthood   as judged so by your lords;
Is there here any high man,   haughty earl or another,
Who will thus sally forth   for the love of his Emperor?'   1660

And an earl then, with anger,   answers him swiftly:
'I am angry at Arthur   and at his high nobles
That thus in error   occupies these our realms,
And enrages the Emperor,   his lord on this earth.
The array and the royalty   of the Round Table   1665
Are recalled with rancour   in all of our realms,
Of how they all hold revels   with rents due to Rome;
He shall rue his reasoning,   if right favours us,
And all shall repent   who ride in his retinue
Because of how rashly   their ruler so governs!'   1670

'Ah, so Christ help me!'   says Sir Clegis then,
'I can see by your carping   that you seem an accountant!
But be you auditor or earl   or even the Emperor,
I will answer you thus,   on account of Arthur,
That warrior so regal   who rules all of us   1675
That make up the rich retinue   of the Round Table:
He has reviewed his account   and read all his records,
And will give you this reckoning   which you shall rue later,
That all the rich shall repent   who call themselves Roman
Lest the arrears be repaid   of the rent which he claims.   1680
'We crave of your courtesy   three cracks at this joust;
The winner takes all: and keeps all claims to knighthood!
You try to trick us today   with your trifling words;
I suspect such treachery   as behoves travelling men! †
So send out to us swiftly   the knights you select   1685
Or say to me surely   that you will surrender.'

 'So save me Our Lord,'   says the King of Syria,
'You can stall here all day;   you will see naught delivered †
Unless I be assured   of your knighthood with certainty, †
That your coat and your crest   are recognised by lords   1690
As ancestral arms   that are endowed with lands.'
'Sir King,' says Sir Clegis,   'you ask as a kind knight;
I trust it be for cowardice   that you speak these words;
My arms are of ancestry,   acknowledged by lords,
And borne into battle   since the time of Brutus;   1695
At the city of Troy,   besieged at that time, †

They were often seen in assault   leading matchless knights;
And then Brutus brought us,   and all our bold elders,
To Great Britain the broad   aboard all his ships.'

'Sir,' says Sir Sextynour,   'you can say what you like,   1700
But we shall make you suffer   as best seems to us;
See you truss up your trumpets   and trifle no longer,
For though you tarry all the day,   you will not tide any better,
And never shall any Roman   who rides in my retinue
Be rebuked by such rogues   while I roam on this earth!'   1705

Then Sir Clegis inclined   in a bow to that king,
And canters back to Sir Cador   and courteously tells him:
'We have found in that forest,   with its flourishing leaves,
The fairest flower of folk   that belongs to your foe:
Fifty thousand in force,   all fierce men at arms,   1710
That are fewtered most fine   under yonder free boughs;
On horseback in ambush   with banners displayed
They wait in the beech wood,   upon the wayside.
They hold fast at the ford   where the water is fair
Faithfully in force,   to fight as behoves;   1715
For thus things shape up   and we must shortly say
Whether we shun or show;   we will shift as you wish.'
'Nay,' said Sir Cador,   'so help me Christ,
We should bring ourselves shame   if we shunned a fight!
Lancelot will not laugh at me,   he who lodges with the king,   1720
That I let my way be blocked   by any lord upon earth;
I would be dead and undone   before I dawdle here
For dread of some dog's son   in yonder dim bushes!'

Sir Cador then knightly   comforts his clan
And with keen encouragement,   he speaks these words: 1725
'Think of our valiant prince   who always invests us
With lands and with lordships   wherever we like;
That has dealt out duchies   and dubbed us as knights,
Given us gifts and gold   and granted many rewards –
Greyhounds and great horses   and a good many joys –   1730
Which bring grace to all men   who go forth under God.

Think of the rich renown   of the Round Table:
Let it never be relinquished   to no Roman on earth;
Do not fare faintly   nor fetter no weapon,
But look to fight faithfully,   fierce men that you are;   1735
I would well be boiled quick   and quartered asunder
Than not work my duty   while so full of wrath.'

Then this doughty duke   dubbed his great knights:
Ioneke and Askanere,   Aladuke and others,
Who were heirs of Essex   and all those eastern marches,   1740
Howell and Hardolf   so happy in arms,
    And Sir Heryll and Sir Herygall,   both war-hungry knights.
Then this sovereign assigned   certain of his lords,
Sir Gawain, Sir Uriel,   Sir Bedevere the wealthy, †
Raynald and Richard,   both children of Rowland: 1745
'Keep safe our prisoner   with your prize knights
And if we in the struggle   withstand defeat,
Stay standing right here   and stir no further;
But if by chance we fall,   that we are charged down,
Discharge yourself to some castle,   seek safe charity there   1750
Or ride to our rich king,   without rest if you can,
And bid him come readily   to rescue his retinue.'

And then boldly the Britons   put shield to vambrace,
Don their bright bascinets   and brandish their lances;
Thus he fits out his force   and rides to the field,   1755
Five hundred in a front   with all their lances fewtered!
With trumpets they trot   those steeds in their trappings,
With cornets and clarions   and carefully played notes; †
Shooting in with a shock   they shirk no further,
Where the shrubs all shone   sheltered in the trees.   1760
And then the Roman army   retreats a little,
Those royal knights moved back   towards their rear guard;
So rapidly they ride   that the whole army rings
With riven-wrought steel   and rich gold mail.

Then many schiltrons   shot out from the bushes   1765
With sharp weapons of war,   shooting at once.

84

The King of Libya fronts   the vanguard he leads,
And all his loyal liegemen   cry out aloud.
Then this cruel king   couches his lance;
On his caparisoned steed,   he canters straight on his course.   1770
He bears to Sir Berill   and fiercely strikes a blow
Through the gorget and gullet,   hurting him grievously.
The knight on his great horse   lies gaunt on the ground
And cries gravely to God   and gives Him his soul.
Thus Sir Berill the Bold   is robbed of his life   1775
And bides waiting burial   as is best and seemly.

Then Sir Cador of Cornwall   is downcast in heart
Because of his kinsman   who has been so killed;
He clasps close his corpse   and kisses him often,
And commands his best knights   to keep him protected.   1780
Then the Libyan king laughs,   and mouths out aloud:
'Your lord has alighted!   Me likes this the better!
He will not damage us today;   let the Devil have his bones!'
'That king,' says Sir Cador,   'bombastically speaks,
Because he killed my kinsman: let Christ have your soul! –   1785
He shall have his corn-bote,   so Christ help me!
Before I quit this park,   we shall clash but once:
However wends the wind,   I will reward him by dusk,
Either himself for sure,   or some of his fellows!'
Then Sir Cador the keen,   as becomes a true knight,   1790
Cries out, 'A Cornwall!'   and casts his lance in its fewter,
And on a great steed   strikes straight through the battle;
Many strong men he struck   by his strength alone;
When his spear was split,   he sped on with all eagerness
And swept out his sword   which never forswore him,   1795
Wrought wide ways in swathes   and wounded great knights,
Works thus his own pathway   until his sides were aching
And hews wholly asunder   the hardiest of necks,
Such that all blends with blood   where his horse so barges!
He brought an end to the lives   of many bold nobles,   1800
And topples down tyrants   and empties their saddles,
Then turns from his toils   when he thought the time right!

Then the Libyan king   cries full loud
At Sir Cador the keen   with these cruel words:
'You have won worship   and wounded knights;   1805
You wantonly act   like the world is your own –
I am right here and waiting,   sir, by my word;
Hold yourself forewarned,   you had better beware!'
Commanded by clarion horns,   newly-called knights
Respond to their cry   and cast their lances to fewter,   1810
Charge forth in a front   on steeds like forged iron [†]
And first of all felled   some full fifty at once!
They shot through the schiltrons,   shattered their lances,
Laid down a huge lump   of great lordly men,
And thus nobly our new knights   announce all their strength!   1815
But new nonsense is here   that saddens me greatly.

That Libyan king   takes a steed that he liked
And comes in most lordly   dressed in silver lions,
Launches into the melee   and cleaves it in half;
He steals the lives   of many lords with his lance!   1820
Thus he chases the child-knights   of the king's chamber,
And cheerless in the field   kills chivalrous knights;
With a spear for the chase,   he chops many down! [†]
Sir Aladuke was slain there,   and Sir Achinour wounded,
Sir Origge and Sir Ermyngall   hewn all to pieces!   1825
And they latched hold of Lewlin,   and likewise his brother,
Did those Libyan lords   who led them to their strongholds;
Had Sir Clegis not come,   and Clement the noble,
Many would have been slain   and our new men come to naught.

Then Sir Cador the keen   casts to his fewter   1830
A lance cruel and keen,   and rides to the king,
Hits him high on the helm   with his hard weapon,
Such that all his hot blood   runs right down to his hands!
That hot-headed heathen   now lies on the heath,
And he was never healed   of his mortal hurt!   1835
Then Sir Cador the keen   cries out full loud:
'You have your corn-bote, Sir King,   may God be kind in His
    mercy;

You killed my blood-cousin   so I could not care less!
Cool yourself in the clay   and comfort yourself!
You have long scorned us   with your scornful words,   1840
So now you have secured   these scars in reward!
Have what you would harvest,   it harms us but little,
For scorn haunts the home   of he who would use it.'

Then the King of Syria   is full of great sorrow
For the sake of his sovereign   who was thus so slain;   1845
He assembled his Saracens,   and many senators,
And savagely they set   on diverse of our knights.
    Sir Cador of Cornwall   swiftly counters them
With his kindred company   all cleanly arrayed;
At the front of the forest,   as that way goes forth,   1850
A full fifty thousand folk   were felled all at once! †
There were many strong knights   in that vast onslaught
Who were soon wounded sorely   upon every side;
The strongest of the Saracens,   steadfast in allegiance,
Were sat in their saddles   some six feet above;   1855
They smashed many schiltrons   of shielded knights;
Shot through many sure soldiers   with shining mail;
They pierced many a breast   through well-bound byrnies;
And they burst asunder   well-burnished bracers,
Bloodied great blazons   and hewed at broad horses   1860
With blades of bright steel,   making steeds bridle!
Those Britons boldly   batter so many
That the broad field and boulders   all run with blood!
By then, keen Sir Kay   has captured a captain,
And Sir Clegis clatters in   and catches another,   1865
The Captain of Cordewa   who, apart from the king, †
Was key to the country   along all that rich coast.
Ioneke had ensnared   Utolf and Evander
With the Earl of all Africa   and other great lords.

The keen King of Syria   yields now to Sir Cador;   1870
The Seneschal of Sutri   so too to Sagramour.
When that chivalrous host   saw their chieftains were
        taken,

They choose their own way   chiefly to the deep forest,
And they felt so faint   that they fall in the groves
In the ferns of that forest   for the fear of our forces.   1875
There might men see our royalty   ride in the shrubs
To rip up the Romans   all wounded and ruddy;
Shouting after those men,   hot-tempered knights,
They hewed them down by the hundred   by the holt-side!
Thus our chivalrous men   chase all those people;   1880
A few who escaped   scattered back to a castle.

Then the Round Table   rallies its ranks
So to ride through the woods   where the Duke rests;
They run round through trees   and retrieved all their friends
Who were all fallen dead   from the fighting before.   1885
Sir Cador ordered them carried   away under fine covers
And taken straight to the king   by his unequalled knights;
And he passes towards Paris   with the prisoners himself,
Entrusted them to the Provost,   those princes and others,
Takes supper in the great tower   and tarries no longer   1890
But quick returns to the King   and tells him with his tongue:

 'Sire,' says Sir Cador,   'this case so befell us:
We encountered today   in your rich country,
Both kings and kaisers,   cruel and noble,
And knights and keen men   all cleanly equipped!   1895
They had in that forest   forestalled us on our way,
With fierce men at arms   by a ford in that forest;
There we fought faithfully,   fighting with spears,
And felled all your foes   as they stood in the field.
The Libyan king is laid low,   left on that ground fallen,   1900
And many of his liegemen   that were loyal to him;
Other lords are all caught   from lands unfamiliar;
We have led them to long here   to do with what you like.
Sir Utolf, Sir Evander,   those honourable knights,
Ioneke has captured,   by craft of arms,   1905
And earls of the Orient   and many strong knights,
The best men by lineage   who belonged to that host;
Barouns the Senator   is caught by a knight;

That most cruel Captain   of Corneto is held;
The Seneschal of Sutri,   hostile like these others: 1910
The King of Syria himself   and countless Saracens.

'But fourteen of our knights   are fallen in the field.
I will not refrain nor defer   from telling you faithfully;
Sir Berill is one,   that noble banneret,
Killed in the first action   by a royal king;   1915
     Sir Aladuke of Towell,   with his tender knights,
Was taken by Turks   and in time was found felled;
And good Sir Mawrelle of Mawnces   and Mawrene his brother,
Sir Meneduke of Mentoche   and his marvellous knights.'

Then that worthy king writhes,   and wept with his eyes, 1920
And speaks these words   to his cousin Sir Cador:
'Sir Cador, your courage   confounds us all!
You have cost me through cowardice   the cream of my
          knights!
To put men in peril   is no prize achievement
Unless the parties are prepared   and powerfully arrayed;   1925
When you were stationed strongly   you should have stayed put,
Rather than destroy at once   all my strongest men!'

'Sir,' says Sir Cador,   'you know well yourself
That you are king of this country   and can speak as you like!
But no noble of your Table   shall ever upbraid me   1930
That I boast and brag   rather than do your bidding;
So when men start on campaign   supply them with stout stuff
Lest they be astonished   and destroyed in strange lands.
I did my duty today –   I will be judged by your lords –
And was in danger of death   from diverse knights.   1935
Yet you grace me with no grandeur,   only grave words;
But though my heart is heavy,   I will not hide what has happened.'

Though Sir Arthur was angered,   he answers fairly:
'You have done doughty deeds,   Sir Duke, with your hands,
And have done your duty   with my dear knights;   1940
Therefore you are deemed,   by dukes and earls,

As one of the doughtiest   that ever was dubbed!
I am without issue,   childless on this earth;
You are my heir apparent,   as might be one of your children,
You are the son of my sister;   I shall never forsake you!'†   1945

Then he ordered a table   set in his own tent,
And summoned with trumpets   those exhausted knights,
And served them solemnly   with spectacular dishes;
A most seemly sight   on their silver salvers.

Elsewhere, when the senators   heard what had happened,   1950
They said to their Emperor,   'Your soldiers were surprised!
Your enemy, Sir Arthur,   has overthrown those lords
Who rode to the rescue   of those royal knights!
Time is of the essence,   do not torment your people;
Your men have betrayed you   who you trusted the most.   1955
This will turn into torture   and trouble you for ever!'
Then the Emperor was irate   and angry at heart,
At our valiant nobles   who had won such prowess.
So he goes to counsel   with his kings and kaisers,
Sovereigns and Saracens   and many senators.   1960
He assembles full soon   certain of his lords
And in the assembly,   he says these words to them:
'My heart most truly is set,   should you please assent,
To advance into Soissons   with my surest knights,
And fight with my foe,   if fortune allows,   1965
In all four earthly quarters   where that fellow may be found;
Or to enter Autun   in pursuit of adventure, †
And bide with my bold men   within that royal borough,
Resting and revelling,   all riotous together,
Longing there in delight   in its plentiful lordships,   1970
Until Sir Leo is come   with all his loyal knights,
And the lords of Lombardy   to forestall my foe.'

But our wise king is wary,   keeping watch for those
                warriors,
And wisely withdraws   his host from the woods;
He orders false campfires be fed,   flaming full high,   1975

And his men to truss packs   and then retreat in secret.
Then swiftly he goes   in haste towards Soissons,
And at the sun rise   he separates his knights:
He encircles the city   on several flanks,
Swiftly on each side   at seven great stations,   1980
And also in the valley   where his vanguard waits hidden.
Sir Valiant of Wales,   with his valiant knights,
Made several vows   before the face of the king,
To vanquish by victory   the Viscount of Rome!
And so the king chooses him,   as chance befalls,   1985
To be chief of the charge   with his chivalrous knights,
And makes this known by mouth   to those he most trusts;
He will most honourably   command the middle ward,
And form up his foot soldiers   as best he thinks fit;
At the front, in the fore ward,   stand the flower of his knights.   1990
He then orders his archers   to form on either flank,
And shape up by the schiltrons   to shoot when so ready; †
He arrayed in the rear ward   his most royal knights,
The most renowned ranks   of the Round Table:
Sir Raynald, Sir Richard,   who would never run,   1995
The rich Duke of Rouen   with riders aplenty;
Sir Kay, Sir Clegis   and capable knights,
The king commands keep watch   by the clear waters.
Sir Lot and Sir Lancelot,   those lordly knights,
Shall lie on the left   with enough legions   2000
To move in the morning   if mists descend;
Sir Cador of Cornwall,   and his keen knights,
Will keep watch at the crossroads   close to the others;
Thus he puts, in such places,   princes and earls
So no party should pass   by no private way.   2005

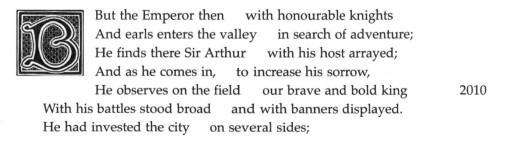

But the Emperor then   with honourable knights
And earls enters the valley   in search of adventure;
He finds there Sir Arthur   with his host arrayed;
And as he comes in,   to increase his sorrow,
He observes on the field   our brave and bold king   2010
With his battles stood broad   and with banners displayed.
He had invested the city   on several sides;

Men were clad in arms   about clough and cliff,
And by moss and by marsh   and on mountains high
Were men in great multitude   to harm him if he came!   2015

When Sir Lucius sees him   he says to his lords:
'This traitor has travelled   here to work treason!
He has surrounded this city   on several sides,
And on its cloughs and the cliffs   with cruel men-at-arms!
There is no way, I would say,   nor no other choice   2020
But to fight with our foe   since we can never flee!'
Then this regal man   arrays his troops rapidly
And thus arranged his Romans   and his royal knights:
The Viscount of Rome   has control of the vanguard
With valiant knights   from Viterbo and Venice   2025
All dressed up and dreadful   below a gold dragon,
With eagles enamelled   all over in black;
They draw wine solemnly now   and drink it in draughts,
Did those redoubtable peers,   dukes and dubbed knights;
With German dancing   and the din of loud pipes,†   2030
That din rang even louder   in the dale where they lodged.

 And then Sir Lucius aloud   said these lordly words:
'Think on the great renown   of your royal fathers,
Those Roman ravagers   who ruled with their lords,
And whose ranks overran   all those who reigned on earth, 2035
    Conquered all Christendom   by craft of arms;
In every adventure   they were held victorious,
Unseated every Saracen   within seven winters
In that part from Port Jaffa   to the gates of Paradise!
If realms be rebellious,   we reckon it but little   2040
To act with right reason   to restrain their ranks!
Thus, do let us dress   and bide here no longer
For doubtless indeed   this day shall be ours!'

When these words were spoken,   the Welsh king himself
Rounded on that warrior   who would war with his knights;   2045
Bravely in that valley   he cries with his voice:
'Oh, Viscount of Valence,   who envies great deeds,

Today I shall avenge   your villainy at Viterbo! [†]
I will neither be vanquished   nor vanish in flight.'
Then in noble voice,   the valiant Viscount   2050
Advanced from the vanguard   and ventured round on his horse;
He dressed in a bold shield   indented with sable
And with a dragon engorged   in most dreadful display,
Devouring a dolphin   with doleful looks,
As a sign that our sovereign   should be destroyed,   2055
And all done of his days   by deadly sword strokes,
For there is naught but death   where that dragon is raised! [†]

Then the comely king   casts in his fewter
His cruel lance   and strikes his foe exactly
A hand-span by the waist,   splitting the short ribs,   2060
So both steel plates and spleen   all cling to the spear!
The blood spurted and spread   as the horse springs,
And he sprawls with speed to the soil,   but he speaks no more!
And thus has Sir Valiant   held to his vows
And vanquished that Viscount,   who was once the victor!   2065

Then Sir Ewain Fitz Urien   rides in fast and eager
Towards the Emperor   to grasp his eagle;
He bustles with haste   through the broad battle,
Brings out his bright sword,   and with a blithe cheer,
Readily arrests it   and rides away   2070
With that fowl for his fare   in his fair hands
And freely falls back   in the front with his brothers.

Now Sir Lancelot bustles up,   bringing himself
To Sir Lucius the lord   and loathsomely strikes him;
He pierced the paunce   and the plate and the mail   2075
Such that his proud pennon   perches in his paunch!
The head hailed out behind,   more than half a foot,
That hard weapon had cut   through hauberk and haunch;
He strikes to the ground   that strong man from his steed,
Struck down a standard   and strolls back to his men!   2080

'I like this much,' says Sir Lot,   'that those lords are defiled!
It is my own lot,   with the leave of my lord,
That my name be laid low,   and my life hereafter,
Unless they lose the living   which they leach from your lands!'
Then that stout one stretches   and strains his bridle,   2085
Strikes into the struggle   on a great steed,
Joins quick with a giant   and jagged him right through!
This gentle knight joyfully   out-jousted another,
Wrought great wide ways,   worrying those knights,
And wounds all woefully   that stand in his way!   2090
He fights with his foes   for a furlong or more,
Felled many on that field   with his fair weapon,
Victoriously vanquished   many valiant knights
And ventured right round the valley,   to leave it when he liked! †

Thereafter most boldly,   the bowmen of Britain   2095
Battled with brigands   from afar in those lands,
With fleet flying arrows,   they shot fresh at those fellows;
Those feather-fletched shafts   pierced through the fine mail;
Such warfare is foul   that so hurts the flesh
Of the flanks of great steeds   when fought from afar!   2100
Then Germans dealt darts   in due response,
With dreadful dings of death   like daggers through shields;
With quaint cunning, their quarrels   cut through our knights
With iron more quickly   than one eye could wink. †
Thus they shrunk from the shock   of all those sharp arrows,   2105
So that their schiltrons shunted   and shuddered as one!
Even great steeds rear up   and their riders crash down,
So that one hundred high men   now lie on the heath.
Then the highest on high,   heathens and others,
Hurtle over that host   to work their harm.   2110
And all these jumping giants,   engendered by fiends,
Join battle with Sir Jonathal   and his gentle knights;
With clubs of clean steel,   they clanged at helmets,
Crashed at many crests   and crushed brains of men,
Killed many coursers   and armour-clad steeds,   2115
Chopped through chevaliers   on chalk-white chargers;
Neither steel nor steed   could stand against them,

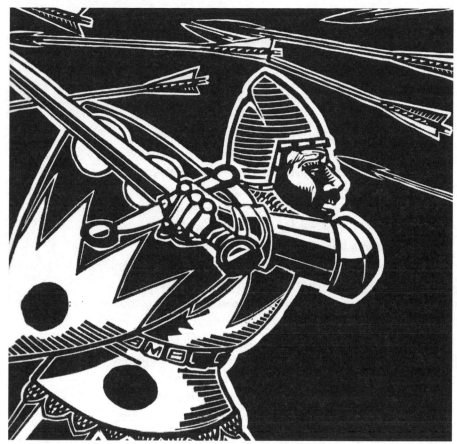

With fleet flying arrows,   they shot fresh at those fellows;
Those feather-fletched shafts   pierced through the fine mail

They astonish and strike down   all who stood in their way.
Then the Conqueror came,   with his keenest knights,
And with his cruel countenance,   he cried full loud: 2120
'I never thought that no Briton   would be so much abashed
As by these bare-legged boys   that abound on this field!'

He clutches at Caliburn,   burnished most cleanly,
Gallops over to Golapas,   who grieved him the most,
Cuts him keen through the knees,   both clean asunder;   2125
'Come down here,' said the king,   'and speak to your brothers!
You are too high by half,   I have to say!

You will yet be more handsome,   with the help of our High Lord!' †
And with that steel sword,   he strikes off his head.
Sternly in that struggle,   he strikes another   2130
And then sets on seven more   with his surest knights;
They never stopped till   sixty more were so served!
And so at this joining,   the giants are destroyed,
And on that day just out-jousted   by gentler knights.

Then the Romans and ranks   of the Round Table   2135
Regrouped in array,   their rearward and elsewhere,
Wrought blows on helmets   with weapons of war,
And ripped with strong steel   the most royal of mail.
But these noble fellows,   fit fairly for fighting,
Fewter their lances freely   on iron-fleshed steeds,   2140
Forge forward full fiercely   with flashing spears
And cut off golden frippery   fastened to shields;
So many fell fighting,   left on the field,
That each forest footpath   runs with red blood!
And so swiftly the greensward   sweated with gore;   2145
Swords swung together,   and knights swooned dead,
Wallowing wild and defenceless   on wayward steeds;
Wounded worthy men   worked loose from their sides,
Their faces disfigured,   their matted locks filthy,
Now all crushed and much trodden   by armour-trapped steeds.   2150
The fairest of figures   that ever walked forth?
A thousand were fallen   of them for a furlong!

By then the Romans   were repelled a little,
And drearily withdraw,   delaying no longer;
Our powerful prince   sets off in pursuit,   2155
Picking off the proudest   with his princely knights.
Sir Kay and Sir Clegis,   with clean men of arms,
Encounter them at the cliff   with competent men,
Fight fast at the forest,   forgoing no weapon,
And felled five hundred at once   in the first attack!   2160
And when they found they were fenced in   by our fierce knights –
That so few to so many   they be outfought and felled –
They rallied forth with their spears   to fight that force again,

96

And fought with the fiercest   that belong to France.
Then Sir Kay the keen   casts his lance to the fewter,   2165
Chases out on a courser   and rides to a king;
And with his Lithuanian lance,   he cleaves his sides
So both liver and lungs   dangle down from the lance;
The shaft shot through and shuddered   in that shining byrnie
And shattered that shield   to rest hushed in that man.   2170
But when Sir Kay attacked,   he was caught unawares
By a cowardly knight   of some kingly clan;
When his back was turned,   that traitor struck him
In through the fillets   and so through his flank
Such that the brutal lance   pierced his bowels   2175
And burst them in that brawl   before breaking in two.
Sir Kay knew acutely   from this cruel wound
That he was doomed to death   by that deadly dealt blow;
So he rides in array,   right through the ranks,
Towards that rich warrior   to deal out revenge: 2180
'Take care, you coward,'   he calls at him quickly
And cleaves him clean asunder   with his sparkling sword:
'Had you dealt your death blow   more fairly by hand,
I would have forgiven you my end,   by Christ now in Heaven!' †
He wends to his wise king   and with reverence requests: 2185
'I am woefully wounded,   and will not recover;
Work now to my honour   as duty would ask
And bring me a fair burial,   I bid you no more!
Greet well my lady, the Queen,   if luck wills you live,
And all those beautiful ladies   who belong to her bower;   2190
And my worthy wife,   who never made me wrathful,
Bid her to work for my soul   through her worshipful prayers!'

The confessor to the king   comes, carrying the Host,
To console the knight   and clean him of his sins;
The knight crouched on his knees,   courageous in heart,   2195
And came to his Creator   who comforts us all.

Then with a heart-rending cry,   that rich king for sorrow
Rides into the rout   to revenge this death. †
He pressed into the pack   and meets with a prince,

That was heir to all Egypt   and those eastern marches,   2200
And cleanly cleaves him   asunder with Caliburn!
He bores clean through that noble   and breaks through his saddle,
So that his burst bowels   daubed the back of his horse!
Melancholic but still manly,   he meets with another –
A mighty man in the midst   who angered him most –   2205
And cuts through the mail,   splits his middle asunder,
So all up from his stomach   simply falls from his mount;
The other half of his haunches   were left on his horse;
My hope, true to say,   is his wound never heals!
He shot through the schiltrons   with his sharp weapon,   2210
Sheer slashing through soldiers   and shattering mail;
He brought down banners   and he burst fine shields
Boldly with bright steel   and wreaking his fury;
Wrathfully twisting   by way of his strength,
He worries these foes   and wounded great knights,   2215
Thrust through their midst,   some thirteen times,
And thoroughly thereafter   charges on through the throng!

Then good Sir Gawain   with his gallant knights
Wends in with the vanguard   by the wood side,
Aware that Sir Lucius   was lurking right there   2220
With his lords and liegemen,   all loyal to him.
Then frankly the Emperor   asks of him eagerly:
'Gawain, what do you want?   Work for your weapon?
I would think by your wavering   you want only sorrow;
Wretch, for all your great words,   I will wreak my revenge!'   2225
He takes out his long sword   and quickly lashed out,
And strikes at Sir Lionel   lordly in the field,
Hits him on the head   such that his helm bursts,
And hews into his skull   more than half a hand deep!
Thus he lays into them all   and lordly served them,   2230
He worthily wounded   those worshipful knights!
He fights with Sir Florent,   the finest of swordsmen,
Till the foaming blood   runs fast to his fist!

Then the Romans all rallied   who were so rebuked,
And riding on rested steeds   scattered our men;   2235

For they see their chieftain   all challenged so sorely,
They chase and chop down   our most chivalrous knights!
Sir Bedevere was run through   and his breast burst
With a brutal sword   brandished with a broad hilt;
The right royal steel   runs to his heart   2240
And he drops to the earth;   no sorrow was greater!

Then the Conqueror took heed   and comes with his knights
To rescue the rich men   of the Round Table,
And confront the Emperor,   if luck would permit –
Even reach his eagle –   and he screams out, 'Arthur!'   2245
The Emperor eagerly   then strikes at Arthur
He hits him awkwardly,   and breaks his visor!
The naked sword   annoys his nose sorely;
The blood of that bold king   runs over his breast
And bloodied his broad shield   and his bright mail!   2250
Our bold king turns his horse   by the bright bridle,
And with his busy broadsword   brings down such a blow
Through the byrnie and breast   with his bright weapon
That he slits his throat a-slant   and slays him at once!

Thus ends the Emperor   at the hands of Arthur,   2255
And all his austere host   were then much afraid.

Now those few that are left   fare to the forest
By the fresh water strands   for fear of our folk;
The flower of our fierce men   on ferrous-grey horses
Follow those fellows fiercely   who once were so fearless.   2260

Then our kindred Conqueror   calls out aloud:
'Cousin of Cornwall,   make sure you take care
That no captain cheats death   by consignments of coin
Till that of Sir Kay   is full cruelly avenged!' †
'None shall,' says Sir Cador,   'so Christ help me!   2265
There is no kaiser nor king   who reigns under Christ
That I will not kill cold dead   by the craft of my hands!'
Now might men see chieftains   on their chalk-white steeds
Chop down noble chivalry   deep in the chase;

The richest of Romans   and royal kings   2270
Had ribs ripped asunder   by robust bright steel,
And all their brains burst apart   in their burnished helms,
Butchered by sword blades   abroad in those lands.

They hewed down heathen men   with their hilted swords
By whole hundreds at once   by the holt sides!   2275
There no silver might save them,   nor bring to them succour,
Neither Sultan nor Saracen   nor Senator of Rome!

Then all the Round Table   rallies its ranks
By the rich river   which runs so fair;
They lodge looking lovely   by those pleasant strands   2280
All those lordly nobles,   on the low ground.
They took to their camp   whatever they like to claim:
Camels and crocodiles,   and coffers full rich, †
Hacks and hackneys   and horses for war,
Housing and field homes   of heathen kings;   2285
They rounded up dromedaries   of sundry lords,
And milk-white mules   and most marvellous beasts
Like Elfaydes, fine Arabs   and noble elephants
Which kings of honour   own in the Orient.

So then Sir Arthur   advances thereafter   2290
Along to the Emperor,   with honourable kings;
He had him lifted lovingly   by his lordly knights
And conveyed to the lodgings   where the king himself lies.
Then heralds most highly,   at behest of their lord,
Went hunting for heathens   left dead on the heath;†   2295
The Sultan of Syria   and certain kings,
And sixty of the chief   senators of Rome.
Then they bustle to embalm   those great noble kings,
And swathed them in sendal,   some sixty layers thick;
Then they lagged them in lead,   lest that they should   2300
Chafe, or heat change them,   before they achieve
Their homecoming in Rome,   carried in caskets,
With their banners above,   their badges below,
So that all knights could see,   in each country crossed,

Each king by his colours   and from what land he comes. [†]   2305

And so, on the second day,   soon before dawn,
Two senators come there,   and certain knights,
From the heath, without hoods,   and from near the holt side,
Barefoot on the field,   bearing bright swords,
And bow low to the bold king   before offering their hilts.   2310
To be hanged or beheaded   or hold on to their lives?
Not knowing, they kneeled   before that king in kirtles;
And with careful courtesy   they spoke these words:
'We are two senators,   your subjects from Rome,
Who have saved our lives   by these salty shores;   2315
We hid in the high woods   through the help of Christ;
We beseech your succour,   as our sovereign and lord;
Grant us life and limb   with a charitable heart
For the love of He   who lets you be lord here.'
'I grant,' said the good king,   'by my own grace,   2320
You your life and limb   and leave to pass
And so take my terms   most honourably to Rome;
To that ilk I charge you   before all my chief knights.'
'Yes,' say the senators,   'we shall ensure this;
Solemnly we swear   to do what you say.   2325
We shall linger with no lord   that lives here on earth,
Neither pope nor potentate   nor noble prince;
We will loyally relay   your letters without let
Of no duke nor head peer   upon pain of death!'

Then the bannerets of Britain   bore them to some tents   2330
Where barbers were brought   bearing basins aloft;
In this way with warm water,   they wet them quickly
And shaved them for their mission,   most surely to show
     That these Romans are marked   as recreant and servile;
And so shaven they showed   the great shame of Rome.   2335
Then they quickly coupled   the caskets to camels
And asses and Arabs,   all bearing great kings;
The Emperor, for honour,   was borne on his own
Aloft on an elephant,   his eagle above;
The king consigned them   to the captives himself,   2340
And before all his keen men   he spoke these words:

101

'Here are the caskets,' said the king,   'to carry over the mountains,
Crammed full of the money   which you have much craved,
The tax and the tribute   of ten score winters
That was tearfully taken   in the time of our elders;   2345
    Say to the senator   who controls that city
That I send him this sum   to assess how he likes!
But bid him never be so bold,   while those of my blood reign,
To come battling again   for all my broad lands,
Nor seek tax nor no tribute   nor no kind of title,   2350
Lest he wants more of such treasure,   while my time lasts!'

Now they ride to Rome   by the readiest ways;
Bells clang in the Capitol   to summon the Commons
And sovereigns and senators   who rule that city.
They committed their carriages,   caskets and more,   2355
As the Conqueror had commanded,   repeating his cruel words:
'We have trustfully travelled   to fetch here these takings,
The tax and the tribute   of four score winters, †
Of England and Ireland   and their outer isles,
Occupied as his own   in the Occident by Arthur.   2360
He bids you never be so bold,   while those of his blood reign,
To battle for Britain   nor his broad lands,
Nor seek tax nor no tribute   nor no kind of title
Save such treasure as this   while his time lasts.
We have fought in France   and foul things have hurt us,   2365
And many of our fair folk   are believed fallen dead!
No chieftain or chivalry   achieved an escape
But, as chance so befalls,   were chopped down in the chase!
We say ready your stone stores,   strengthen your walls;
Woe and war you have woken;   beware as you will!'   2370

When May comes in the calendar,   the following occurs:
The renowned royal king   of the Round Table
Since his taking the shores   on the coast of Cotentin,
Has rebuked those rich Romans   once and for all!
    So when he had fought in France   and won all the field   2375
And felled with ferocity   all his foes there,
He bides for the burials   of his bold knights,

102

Who were robbed of their lives   by sword blades in battle.
He buries at Bayonne   Sir Bedevere the rich;
He leaves at Caen   the corpse of Kay the keen,   2380
Covered with crystal,   cleanly all over;
Because his own knightly father   had conquered that country. †
Then he bided in Burgundy   to bury more knights,
Sir Berade and Baldwin,   and regal Sir Bedwar,
Then Sir Kay at Caen,   as is most kindly asked.†   2385
And so in August,   King Arthur thereafter
Enters all Germany   with his host arrayed,
Then lingers at Luxembourg   to let all his knights heal,
With his loyal liegemen,   as rightful lord here.
And on the Day of Saint Christopher,   he calls a counsel   2390
With kings and kaisers,   clerks and others,
And keenly commands them   to guide him with care
How he may conquer by craft   the country he claims.
Thus the keen Conqueror,   with noble courtesy,
Speaks in his counsel,   declaring most knightly: 2395
'A knight keeps these cloughs,   enclosed by hills,
That I am keen to counter   on account of his deeds;
He is liege lord to Lorraine;   I will not conceal it; †
The lordship is lovely,   I am led to believe.
I will divide that duchy   as I choose to do,   2400
And then deal with that Duke   if destiny permits;
He has been a rank rebel   to my Round Table,
And always ready with Rome   to run riot in my lands!
We shall reckon with wrath,   if reason so happens,
Who has the right to those revenues,   by revered God of Heaven! 2405
'Then I will like to go   and show myself in Lombardy,
And set laws in that land   that shall last for ever;
I will test a little   those tyrants of Tuscany –
But only in matters temporal –   while my time lasts;
I will give my protection   to all Papal lands,   2410
Showing the people   my rich pennon of peace.
It is folly to offend   our Father under God,
Either Peter, or Paul,   the apostles of Rome;
If we spare those who are spiritual   success will be ours;
Thus while we can still speak,   none shall be despoiled!'   2415

Now they speed at their spurs,   without any more speaking,
Do these manly knights,   to the marches of Metz,
That is as lauded in Lorraine   as London is here,
And where sits that sire   who lords there as sovereign.
The king forges forward   on a fair steed   2420
With Ferrar and Ferraunt   and four other knights;
And next, those seven   all circled that city
To seek the safest places   to set their siege engines.
Then those sat in the city   bent back their stout crossbows
And shot bolts at that bold king   with bitter intent;   2425
Those eager arbalesters   aimed right at King Arthur
To hurt him or his horse   with their hateful weapons.
Yet the king shunned no shot,   no shield he sought,
But shows up all shining   in shimmering clothes,
Longs there at his leisure   and looks at the walls,   2430
To seek the lowest place   where his lords could assail.
'Sire,' says Sir Ferrar,   'you work but pure folly,
To ride like a noble   near these walls yet so naked, †
In your surcoat so singular   to survey this city
And by such showing off   to bring shame on us all.   2435
Hence let us move hastily   lest foul things may happen,
For it harms us for ever   if they hit you on your horse.' †
'If you are afraid,' said the King,   'then pray ride farther out
Lest they bring you sorrow   with all their round bows.
You are naught but an infant,   I think it fair to say!   2440
You would flee from a fly   that lands on your flesh!
I am aghast at no thing,   so help me Lord God!
If those gadlings be grievous,   they grieve me but little;
They will not win my renown   but just waste all their tackle;
I shall wend where I want,   I will wager my head!   2445
Those hounds will have no such luck,   with the help of my Lord,
As to kill a crowned king   anointed with chrism!'

Now come our head scouts,   battle-hardened knights,
Given heart by the whole host   which hurries behind;
And our fierce foragers   from several flanks   2450
Fly quick to the front   on ferrous-grey steeds;
Forging forth in array   now come those regal knights,

That well-renowned retinue   of the Round Table!
All the fierce men of France   followed thereafter
To the front in their finery   and form up on the field.   2455
Then those chevaliers   shift their horses sharply,
To show themselves and display   all their shining apparel; †
They bustle in their battle   with banners displayed,
Bearing their broad shields   and their noble helmets,
And pennons and pennants   with the arms of each prince   2460
All resplendent with pearls   and precious stones;
The lances with their flags   and gleaming shields
Flashed as like lightning,   and gleamed all over.

 Then these prize men prick spurs   and press their horses
        forward
And descend on the city   upon several sides;   2465
First they search in the suburbs,   to be sure and safe,
Discover crossbowmen   and skirmish a little,
Scare their shield-bearers   and their scuffling scouts,
Break down their barricades   with their bright weapons,
Beat down a barbican   and win the bridge;   2470
Had not the garrison   been good at the great gates,
Our men would have won it   by sheer strength alone!
Then our men withdraw   to dispose themselves better,
For dread that the drawbridge   should trap them inside; †
They hurry to the high camp   which the king inhabits,   2475
With his retinue and host   all horsed on steeds;
Then the prince was appraised   and places were picked
To pitch silk pavilions   and prepare for a siege.
Then they lodge most lordly,   however they like,
Keep watch in each ward,   as befits such warfare,   2480
And set up and assemble   certain siege engines.

On Sunday as the sun   yields of its first light,
The king calls on Florent,   that flower of knighthood:
'Our Frenchmen grow feeble,   me thinks no fair wonder!
These folk find life hard   in these fair marches;   2485
They cannot find here   the food and flesh they prefer.
Here are fair forests   to be found all around us

In which our foes have fled   and their beasts roam unfettered!
You shall forge to the fells   and forage in the mountains;
Sir Farraunt and Sir Floridas   shall follow your lead.   2490
We must refresh all our people   with some fresh meat,
That feeds in the forest   on the fruits of the earth. †
Sir Gawain himself   will wend with you also,
Our most worshipful warden,   as well seems so fitting;
Sir Wichard, Sir Walter,   these worshipful knights,   2495
With all the wisest men   of the western marches,
Sir Clegis, Sir Claribald,   Sir Cleremond the Noble
And the Captain of Cardiff,   arrayed and equipped.
Go now, warn the watch,   Sir Gawain and others,
And wend forth on your way   without any more words.'   2500

Now these fresh men-at-arms   fare to the forest;
Those fine nobles went   to the colourful fells;
Through vale and hedge,   by high hill and onwards,
Through holts and hoar woods   with groves of hazel,
And through morass and moss   in those high mountains;   2505
Till on that misty morning   they come to a meadow,
Mown, but unmade,   and not much maintained,
And in swathes all scythed down   yet full of sweet flowers;
There these bold men unbridle   their horses to browse.
Then towards the day break   the birds all began to sing   2510
While the sun rises,   which is sent by Christ;
That soothes every sinner   who sees it on earth.

Then the warden wends out,   Sir Gawain himself,
A wise man and strong warrior,   some wonder to seek;
Then he was aware   of a wondrous armed man,   2515
Baiting him on the riverbank   by the edge of the wood,
Bedecked in a byrnie,   bright to behold,
Bearing a broad shield   on a noble horse,
With no obedient squire,   save but a boy,
Who rests nearby on a horse   and holds his spear.   2520
His shield was graced with three greyhounds   of black, couchant
     on gold,

Wearing chokers and chains   of chalk-white silver;
A gem of changeable hues   was charged on its chief;
And a bold chief he was,   challenging all to attack him! †

Sir Gawain beholds the man   with great gladness of will!   2525
He grips in his hand   a great spear from his groom,
Rides straight over the stream   on his fine steed,
Advances bold and steadfast   towards that strong knight
And eagerly shouts out,   'Arthur' in English!
The other, incensed,   soon answers him,   2530
Replying all loud   in the tongue of Lorraine
Such that all lords might hear him   more than a mile off!
'What pricks you, pilferer,   who proffers me battle?
You have picked your prey poorly   for all your great pride,
For you are imperilled   lest you put up good fighting   2535
And you shall be my prisoner   for all your pompous looks!'
'Sir,' says Gawain,   'so help me God,
Gormless braggarts like you   do not gall me one bit!
But if you grab your gear,   then you will meet grief
Before you go from this grove,   for all your great words!'   2540

Then these lordly nobles   take hold of their lances,
Level their long spears   athwart their light-grey steeds,
Clash with adventure   and great craft of arms
Such that both those cruel spears   break apart at once!
They shot through shields   and sheared through chain mail,   2545
And both sheer through the shoulders   a sure hand-span deep!
Thus both of these warriors   are worthily wounded,
Yet they will not retreat   till they wear out their wrath!
Then they grab at their reins   and they ride again;
Readily in a rush   these men draw their swords rapidly,   2550
Heartily hit   great dents on their helmets
And hew at hauberks   with weapons most hard!
Full stoutly they strike,   these stalwart knights,
Stoking at stomachs   with their steely points,
Fighting with a flourish   with their flaming swords   2555
Till the flashes of fire   seemed like flames on their helms!

Then Sir Gawain was aggrieved   and greatly angered;
With Galuth, his good sword,   he grimly strikes
And cleaves clean asunder   the shield of that knight!
Who should look to his left side,   when his horse lunges by   2560
In the clear light of day,   might well see his liver!
Then that great one groans   with grief at his wounds
And aggrieves Sir Gawain,   as he gallops past,
With a slantwise blow   which smites him most sorely;
He hacks asunder   an enamelled ailette,   2565
Bursts open the rerebrace   with his bright sword,
And hacks off the couter   with the clean edge,
Against the vambrace   all veiled with silver!
Through a double vesture   of the richest velvet
He has severed a vein   with that venomous sword,   2570
Which vomits so violently   that all his wits change!
The visor, the aventail   and all his rich vestments
Were varnished all over   with his valiant blood.
Then this tyrant tightly   turns about with his bridle
And talks without tenderness   and says, 'You are touched!   2575
You need a blood bandage,   lest that you blanch,
For all the barbers of Britain   will not staunch your blood; †
He whom this blade has blemished   will never stop bleeding!'

'Yah!' said Gawain,   'you grieve me but a little.
You think to bring terror   on me with your taunts;   2580
You trust my heart falters   with all of your talk?
Trouble will entail,   if you turn from here now;
Unless you tell me tightly,   and not tarry longer,
What may staunch this blood   that thus runs so fast.'
'This I shall tell you solemnly,   I swear it is so;   2585
No surgeon from Salerno   can otherwise save you,
Unless you speak of how   your Christ can save me too,
And quickly shape me for death   by showing me confession.'

'Yes,' said Sir Gawain,   'so help me God,
I will grant you this grace,   though you have grieved me,   2590
If you will speak honestly   of what you seek here,
Singly and singular,   yourself all alone,

108

'My name is Sir Priamus,   my father is a prince,
Praised and approved   by all kings in his province'

And what religion you follow –   conceal nothing with lies –
And what land you rule   and to whom you are loyal.'

'My name is Sir Priamus,   my father is a prince,   2595
Praised and approved   by all kings in his province;
His holdings are rich   in his Roman realms;
He has been a rebel to Rome,   ridden over their lands, †
Waging war wisely   for winters and years
By wit and by wisdom,   with the strength of a warrior,   2600
He has won all he owns   through war fought with honour. †
His blood is of Alexander,   overlord of all kings,

109

His family and lineage   includes Hector of Troy. [†]
I come from this kindred   and also claim descent
From Judas and Joshua,   those most gentle knights;[†]   2605
I am his heir apparent,   and eldest of my kin;
Of Alexandria in Africa,   and all those lands out afar,
I have full possession   and plainly complete control.
In all those precious cities   which pertain to that port,
I shall have truly   the treasure and tithes   2610
And both tribute and tax   while all my time lasts.
I was so haughty at heart,   while I longed at home,
That no man under heaven   reached more than my hip height;
Hence I was sent here   with seven score knights
To be tested in war   by assent of my father;   2615
And I am for my surquedry   shamefully ambushed
And outfought in arms,   disgraced for all time!
Now I have spoken   of the kin that I come from,
Will you speak, out of knighthood,   and confess who you are?'

'By Christ,' quipped Sir Gawain,   'I do not call myself knight![†]   2620
I am but a knave from the quarters   of my king the Conqueror
And have worked in his wardrobe   for winters and years
For long days on his armour   till it was to his liking!
I pitch all the pavilions   which append to him,
Dress dukes and earls   in their chosen doublets,   2625
And attire King Arthur   with his own aketon,
That he has used in war   all these last eight winters!
Yet at Yuletide with great gifts,   he made me a yeoman;
With one hundred pounds   and a horse richly harnessed.
If luck happens to heal me   to stay in his high service,   2630
Then my healing will hasten,   I can honestly tell you!'

'If his knaves are like this,   then his knights must be noble!
No king under Christ   can take him in combat!
He will be heir to Alexander,   who all the world lauded,
Abler than ever was   Sir Hector of Troy!   2635
By that most sacred chrism   on the day of your Christening,
Come, be quick with the truth,   are you called knight or knave?'

110

'My name is Sir Gawain,   I grant you truly,
Cousin of the Conqueror   as he will acknowledge, †
A kindred knight of his chamber,   as his records account;   2640
Most renowned of the Round Table,   as the rolls reveal! †
He dubbed me with his hands   a Duke of the Dozen
Daintily one day,   before all his dear knights;
Grudge me not, good sir,   that this grace becomes me;
It is the gift of God,   and His own to grant!'   2645
'By Peter,' says Priamus,   'now I be better paid
Than if I were both prince   of Provence and rich Paris!
I would personally prefer   to have my heart prised apart
Than be taken prisoner   by any other as his prize.
But nearby is harboured   in those huge holts   2650
Whole battles armed high   – take heed I ask you!
There the dread Duke of Lorraine   lurks with his dearest knights:
The doughtiest of Dauphiné   and untold Germans;
The lords of Lombardy,   all held as great leaders;
The garrison of Mount Gotthard,   all grandly arrayed;   2655
The warriors of Westphalia,   worshipful nobles;
With Saxons and Syrians   and Saracens in numbers;
They are named in the rolls   and number as many
As sixty thousand and ten,   all surely stout men at arms.
Lest you hurry from this heath,   they will harm us both,   2660
For if I am not helped with haste,   I will never be healthy!
Let your henchman take heed   that no horn be blown,
Or I happen that hastily   we will be hewn to pieces;
For nearby is my retinue   who ride where I will them;
There is none more loyal   that rides truly on earth;   2665
Be you caught by those warriors   you will ride no further
And no ransom on earth   will buy you your freedom!' †

Sir Gawain went diverse ways,   lest that woe would come,
With this worthy warrior   who was most sorely wounded.
He marches to the mountain,   to where our men linger   2670
Letting their beasts browse   upon the broad meads;
     There those lords lent low   on their gleaming shields
With loud laughter aloft   for delight at the birds –
The lark and the linnet   which sing lovely songs –

And some were slaked into sleep,   made slumbering people,   2675
By the songs of the season   in that shrub-land all shimmering
Aloud in those hills   with such likeable notes.

Then, Sir Wichard was aware   that his warden was wounded
And went to him weeping   and wringing his hands;
Sir Wichard, Sir Walter,   these wise men-at-arms,   2680
Were worried for Gawain   and went towards him,
Meeting him mid-way;   they thought it marvellous
That he had tamed that man   who seemed so strong and mighty!
For all the wealth of the world   they were never so woeful:
'He whom we all worship   is not long for this world!'   2685

'Do not grieve,' said Gawain,   'for all God's love in heaven,
For these wounds are but gossamer   and given on loan;
Though my shoulder be shredded   and my shield be run through,
And my arm can wield naught   and is unfit for work,
Sir Priamus, this prisoner,   most perilously wounded,   2690
Says that he has the salve   that will save us both.'
Then stern knights step forth   to assist at his stirrups
And their lord alights,   and lets the bridle loose
To let his bold mount   nibble on the bright flowers;
He unties his bascinet,   disrobes of his rich armour   2695
And he bends on his broad shield   and bows to the earth;
In all the body of that bold man   it seems no blood is left!

Then princely knights   press to Sir Priamus
And with due homage, in their arms,   lift him down from his
    horse
And afterwards take off   his helm and his hauberk –   2700
Yet with haste lest his hurt   would cause his heart to fail –
And laid him down on the lawn,   releasing him from his
    armour,
And let him lie lengthways,   as best brought him relief.
A phial of fine gold   they found in his girdle
That is full of the flux   of the four wells   2705
Which flow from Paradise   when the flood rises [†]
And feeds us all   with the fruit it confers;

Be it furbished on flesh   where the sinews are slashed,
Any fellow would be fish-whole   within just four hours! †
They take the clothes from the couple   with clean bare hands;   2710
A calm knight with the clear water   cleanses their wounds,
Kindly cooled them   and comforted their hearts;
And when their cuts were clean,   they clad them again. †
They break open fine barrels   and brought them wine,
The best of roasts and brawn   and the finest of breads;   2715
After they had all eaten,   they armed themselves again.
Then these adventurous men   all cry, 'To arms!'
With clarions clear   all these knights come together,
Calling a counsel   to discuss their case:
'Beyond is a company   of knights all equipped,   2720
The keenest in combat   as live under Christ;
In yonder oak wood   a host is arrayed
Of determined men   from these outer lands,
As Sir Priamus tells us,   so help me Saint Peter!
Go men,' said Gawain,   'and grope in your hearts: 2725
Who shall go to those groves   to seek those great lords?
If we go home with no gains,   the king will be aggrieved
And say we are gadabouts,   aghast at small things!
As so falls on this day,   we are with Sir Florent,
The flower of all France   who flees from nothing;   2730
He was chosen and charged   in the king's own chamber
As chieftain of this challenge,   by noblest chivalry;
So whether he fight or flee,   we will follow him;
I will never forsake him   out of fear of those forces.'

'Fair lord,' says Sir Florent,   'you flatter me finely!   2735
Yet I am but an infant,   not full-tested in arms;
If any folly befall us,   the fault shall be ours,
Forced to flee from France,   and shamed for ever!
Do not knock your renown,   my wit is the weaker,
I say you are our warden;   so we must follow you!   2740
You have forces I say   of not more than five hundred,
And that is fully too few   to fight with them all,
For our horse-folk and handymen   will help us but a little
And they will hurry off in their haste   for all their great words!

I say work with our wits   as wise men of arms   2745
And move wily away   as worshipful knights!' [†]
'Granted,' said Sir Gawain,   'so help me God,
But we are great gallant men   who deserve grand rewards,
The keenest combatants   of the King's chamber,
Who can speak in our cups   the most knightly talk;   2750
Well, we shall prove today   whether we are prize-worthy!' [†]

Now our fierce foragers   ride into the forest
And finding a fair field   alight on foot;
They look for prints of their prey: prized men of arms.
Florent and Floridas,   with five score knights,   2755
Followed into the forest   and found their trail;
Flying at a fast pace,   they rush on their foe.
Then fast on our force   falls well over five hundred
Fierce men from that forest   upon fresh horses;
One Sir Feraunt led them,   upon a fair steed,   2760
Fostered in Famagusta,   the Fiend was his father!
He flies to Sir Florent   and just as fast cries,
'Why flee you false knight?   The Fiend have your soul!'
Then with fervour Sir Florent   casts his lance in his fewter;
On Fawnell of Friesland   he rides to Sir Feraunt[†]   2765
And rattling the reins   of his regal steed,
He rides into the fray,   resting no longer!
Full flat in the forehead   he perforates him,
And all disfigures his face   with his fierce weapon!
Through his bright bascinet,   he has touched his brain   2770
And burst his neck bone   such that all his breath stopped!

Then his cousin exclaimed   and cried full loud:
'You have killed stone-cold dead   the king of all knights!
He who has been field-fettled   in full fifteen realms;
He who found not one fellow   to fight with him alone!   2775
You shall die for this deed   by my own deadly weapon
And your dread knights dealt sorrow   that hide in yonder dale!'

'Fie!' says Sir Floridas,   'you scoffing wretch!
You make for to frighten us,   you fluke-mouthed shrew?'

And, as he glides by,   Floridas with his sword   2780
Flays his foe asunder   with a strike to his flank
So all the filth in that fellow   fell out of his guts,
And foully follows the footsteps   of his horse riding forth!

Then a knight rides forward   to rescue that noble;
This was Raynald of Rhodes,   a rebel to Christ,   2785
Perverted by pagans   who persecute Christians,
Who presses in proudly   in pursuit of his prey,
And who had in Prussia   won praise beyond measure;
His posturing presence   was therefore no surprise!
But then Sir Richard,   a true Round Table knight,   2790
Rides against him   on a great royal steed;
He rushed him so quickly   through his round red shield
That his tempered spear   runs right through his heart!
The knight reels about,   crashes down to the earth
And roars full rudely   but he rode no more!   2795

Now those still fresh and unfallen   of the five hundred
Fall on Sir Florent   and his five score knights,
Between marshland and flood,   upon a flat plain;
Our folk hold fast the field   and fought against them;
Then 'Lorraine!' was cried out,   loud and aloft,   2800
When lords with long spears   crashed all together,
And 'Arthur!' on our side   when danger ailed them.
Then Sir Florent and Floridas   cast their lances to fewter,
Fly fast to the fray   and send fear through those nobles;
They fell five at the front   on their first assault   2805
And then they forge further,   felling many others!
Broad byrnies they burst,   and they broke shields,
And they beat and bear down   on the best who would bother
     them.
All who ruled in that army,   well they ride away –
How rudely they rush,   these right royal knights!   2810

When Sir Priamus, that prince,   perceived their sport
He had pity in his heart   that he dare not take part;
He went to Sir Gawain   and says to him these words:

'Your prized men are pressed sorely   by their own prey;
They are somewhat beset   by seven hundred Saracens,   2815
Knights of the Sultan   from his several lands;
Would you suffer me, Sir,   for the sake of your Christ,
To support them at once   with some of your men?'

'The glory is theirs,' said Gawain,   'I will not begrudge it;
They will have gifts full great,   granted by my lord;   2820
Let the fierce men of France   fettle themselves:
These fellows have not fought   for full fifteen winters!
I will not stir from my stall   by less than half a steed long,
Unless more strife besets them   than just these men on steeds.'

Then Gawain was aware   from without the woods   2825
Of Westphalian warriors,   upon stalwart horses,
Galloping wildly   where that way goes forth,
With every weapon, in truth,   that is wielded in war.
     The old Earl of Antele   advances in the vanguard
With some eight thousand knights   arrayed on either hand;   2830
His pavisers and bowmen   passed all in pure numbers
Than was ever provided   by any prince on earth.

Then the Duke of Lorraine   advances thereafter
With double that number   of bold doughty Germans,
Pagans of Prussia,   noble proud riders,   2835
Who come pressing ahead   with the knights of Priamus.
Then the Earl of Antele   said to Algere his brother:
'The knights of King Arthur   all anger me earnestly,
Who in one eager host   come on our men themselves!
They will soon be undone,   by when undern rings,   2840
Those who come as fools   to fight us all on this field!
I think it fair to say   I fear they will all fall!
Would they renounce their plan   and pass on their way,
Spur home to their prince   and leave off their prey,
They might lengthen their lives   and lose but a little!   2845
It would lighten my heart,   so help me Our Lord!'
'Sire,' says Sir Algere,   'they are somewhat unused
To being outfought in battle: this offends me more!

I say the fairest of our flock   shall be the ones fallen dead,
Before they leave the field,   few though they are!'   2850

Then good Gawain,   gracious and noble,
All glorious with glee   gladdens his knights:
'Good men, be not aghast   at those glittering shields
Though all those gadlings seem gay   on yonder great horses!
Bannerets of Britain,   embolden your hearts!   2855
Let those boys not abash you   with all their bright clothes!
We shall blunt all their boasting   for all of their bluster;
They will submit like a bride   in the bed of her lord! †
The field shall be ours   if we fight today;
Their false faith shall fail,   their falsehood be destroyed!   2860
It seems their folk at the front   are fresh and untested;
Their faith and fealty   is but to the Fiend!
If we venture in battle,   we shall be victorious,
Vaunted by voices   of valiant nobles,
Praised by princes   in the presence of lords,   2865
And loved by ladies   in innumerable lands! †
None of our elders   ever earned such an honour,
Neither Unwin nor Absalom,   nor anyone else! †
When we are in most distress   let us remember Mary,
Who is the saint of our master,   and on whom he trusts much;†   2870
We implore that mild Queen   to commend us all;
Whom so honours that Maid   shall never meet mishap!'

By when these words were said,   they were only apart
By the length of a field   when 'Lorraine' was cried out. †
There was never such jousting   joined in one day on earth –   2875
Judged greater than that   of the Vale of Josephat, †
When Julius and Joatell   met death as their judgement –
As when those regal men   of the Round Table
Rushed right into the fray   on their royal steeds!
For so rapidly they rush   with their spears at the ready   2880
That those rascals were routed   and ran to the woods,
Creeping back to their court,   called cowards for ever!

'By Peter,' said Gawain,   'this gladdens my heart!

Those gadflies are all gone   who gathered in numbers;
I think that those hot heads   will do no further harm   2885
And will hide with full haste   in those holts over there!
They are fewer in the field   than they numbered at first,
By faith all that fair host   is down forty thousand!'
But one Julian of Genoa,   a giant most huge,
Joined battle with Sir Gerard,   a justice of Wales,   2890
Who jags him right through   his gyronny shield
And his fine jazerant   of gentle mail;
Each joint and hinge   he jags right asunder!
He wages war just like this,   on his agile steed,
So that giant is out-jousted –   this wandering Jew –†   2895
And so jocund is Gerard   he could be no more joyous!

Then the genitors of Genoa   joined battle at once
And well over five hundred   force to the front;
A fellow known as Sir Frederick,   with full many others,
Forges forth in a flurry   and cries with fresh feeling   2900
To fight with our foragers   who fare on that field;
And then the royal ranks   of the Round Table
Rode forth with earnest   and ride against them
To melee with the middle ward,   who were not their match;
It was a marvel to hear   the noise of that great multitude!   2905
Then the Saracens discover   in that great assemblage
That the sovereign of Saxony   needed assistance,
His giants out-jousted   by our gentle knights
And being jagged in the heart   through their Genoese jazerants!
They hew through the helmets   of haughty nobles   2910
Such that their hilted swords   run down to their hearts,
And then those renowned ranks   of the Round Table
Rush down and rive through   those renegade wretches;
Thus dukes and earls   are driven to their deaths
By such dreadful deeds   that whole day long!   2915

Then in the presence of lords,   that prince Sir Priamus
Presses to his pennon   and unfurls it openly,
Reversed it readily   and then rides away †
To where the Round Table   was battling in ranks;

And loyally his retinue   rides after him   2920
For they had read his reasoning   by his rich shield.
They shed from that schiltron   like sheep from a fold
And steered forth to the struggle   and stood by their lord!
They then sent a message   to the duke saying this:
'We have been your soldiers   these six years and more,   2925
We forsake you today   and desert to our lord;
We will serve our own sovereign   in several kingdoms.
You have defaulted on our fees   for these past four winters;
You are feeble and false,   spouting naught but fine words,
Our wages have withered   and so too has your war,   2930
We may honourably wend now   wherever we like!
We say you treat for a truce   and trifle no longer
Or you shall loose of your tally   some ten thousand more troops.'

'Fie, damn you,' said the duke,   'the Devil have your bones!
I shall not from you dogs   ever dread any danger!   2935
We shall deal this day,   by deeds of arms,
For my death and my dukedom   and for my dear knights!
I have little esteem   for such soldiers as you
Who claim sudden default   and forsake their lord!' †

The duke dons his shield   and delays no longer,   2940
Draws up a dromedary   with a guard of dread knights,
And gallops to Gawain   with a grand host
Of great men from Grenada,   acknowledged as grievous.
These fresh-horsed men   all ride to the front
And fell at once   some forty of our foragers!   2945
They had fought, for some time,   with over five hundred;
No fair wonder, in faith,   that they felt so faint.
Then Sir Gawain was aggrieved,   he grips his spear
And again gallops in   with his gallant knights,
Meets the Marquis of Metz   and smites him right through –   2950
The man who on middle-earth   had annoyed him the most.
Then one Chastelayne, a child-knight,   of the king's chamber,
A ward to Sir Gawain   in the west marches,
Charges to Sir Cheldrick,   a noble chieftain,
And with a spear for the chase   punctures him through! †   2955

This check he achieved   by pure chance of arms,
So they chase that child,   escape eschewed him,
And one Swyan of Sweden   swung with his sword
And swipes swift asunder   the spine of that squire!
He swooned and died   and fell to the sward,   2960
Swaps life for death swiftly,   to swagger no more!

Then Sir Gawain showed his grief   in his grey eyes;
That young man was good,   a beginner in arms.
Thus, the cheer in his face   changed because of that child
Such that chilling water   ran down his cheeks!   2965
    'Woe is me!' said Gawain,   'that my wits failed to see this!
I shall wager for that one   all the wealth that I wield;
I shall wreak my revenge   on that one who so wounded him!'
With sadness, he arms   and rides to that duke
But one dread Sir Dolphin   advances on him;   2970
Sir Gawain gallops to him   with a grim lance
Such that the ground spear   glided straight to his heart!
And he hauled it out eagerly   and hurt another,
A heathen knight, Hardolf,   a man happy in arms;
Slyly he slits him   through near the breast slot†   2975
So that the sliding spear   slips from his hands!
On that slope is slain,   by the sleight of his hands,
Some sixty sly soldiers   all slung down in a slough!
Though Sir Gawain was woeful,   he waits until
He was aware of that one   who had wounded the child   2980
And with a sword swiftly   he swiped him right through:
His life swept away swiftly,   he swoons to the earth!
And then he runs into the rabble   and rushes on helmets,
He rends rich hauberks   and raised-up shields;
He rides with raging riot   yet keeps a straight road;   2985
Throughout the rear ward   he goes on his way,
Then this rich regal noble   draws in his reins
And rides back to the retinue   of the Round Table.

Then our chivalrous men   all change their horses,
Chase and chop down   great noble chieftains,   2990
Hit full hearty blows   on helmets and shields,

And hurt and hew down   many heathen knights!
The cleave through kettle-hats   right down to the shoulders;
Never was such a clamour   made by captains on earth!
Sons of kings were captured,   courtiers and nobles,   2995
And courtly knights of the kingdom   recognised to be rich;
Lords both of Lombardy   and of Lorraine
Were leashed and led in   by our loyal knights. †
Those who chased that day   never had better chances;
Never once was achieved   such a rich chest from chasing!†   3000

 When Sir Florent had won   the field by force,
He forges forth further   with five score knights;
Their prisoners and plunder   pass on behind,
Kept by bowmen, pavisers   and prize men-at-arms;
Then good Sir Gawain   guides all his knights,   3005
Goes in as best gains him,   as so told by his guides,
So as not to be greeted   by some great lordly garrison
That might grab all his gains   and cause him grief.
Thus they stood in those straits   and paused with his
        soldiers
Till his booty has passed   that path thought most perilous;   3010
Then they see the city   as besieged by their king,
Which will truly by seized   by assault that same day.
A herald is hailed   at the behest of those lords,
Who heads out of the highlands   to that homely camp
And goes fast to the tent   of the king and he tells   3015
All their tale most surely   and how they had succeeded:
'All your foragers are safe   that forayed without,
Sir Florent and Sir Floridas   and all your fierce knights;
They have forayed and fought   with fully great numbers
And felled all your foe-men   and finished their lives!   3020
Our worshipful warden   has wondrously fared,
For he has won today   great immortal renown;
He has slain the Dolphin   and taken the Duke!
Many bold men are dead   by dint of his hands!
He has priceless prisoners,   princes and earls,   3025
Of the richest blood   who reign on earth!
All your chivalrous men   have achieved shining fame,

Monasteries and infirmaries   they hammer to earth,
And churches and chapels,   limed all chalk-white

But Chastelayne, a child-knight,   has been killed by mischance.'
'Hearty man,' says the King,   'Herald, by Christ,
You have healed my heart,   I hereby reward you!   3030
I give you at Hampton   a hundred pound holding!' †

Then the king assembles   all his knights for the assault
With siege towers and sows   upon several sides;
He disperses shield-bearers   and scales the walls
With wise men of arms   awarded to each zone.   3035
        Then boldly they bustle   and bend back siege engines,
Piling them with projectiles   to prove their range.

122

Monasteries and infirmaries   they hammer to earth,
And churches and chapels,   limed all chalk-white.
Stone steeples, once sturdy,   now lie in the streets,   3040
As do chambers and chimneys   of many chief inns,
Their plastered walls pummelled,   despoiled and knocked down;
The pain of the people   was piteous to hear!

Then the duchess dressed   and with her regal damsels,
And the Countess of Crasine   with her maiden company,   3045
Kneel down on the crenels   above where the king rode,
Arrayed most comely   on his caparisoned horse.

'King crowned above all,   kindly hear our plea!
We beseech you, Sire,   as sovereign and lord,
That you save us today   for the sake of your Christ!'

They knew him by his countenance   and cried keen and loud:
'King crowned above all,   kindly hear our plea!
We beseech you, Sire,   as sovereign and lord,   3050
That you save us today   for the sake of your Christ!
Send us some succour,   make peace for my people,
Lest this city be ransacked   in savage assault.' †
He waves up his visor   with a noble flavour
And with virtuous visage,   this valiant lord   3055
Called out most mildly   these comforting words:
'Madam, none of my men   shall misuse you here;
I grant you a peace charter,   and your chief maidens,
Your children, chaste men   and chivalrous knights; †
But the Duke is in danger,   I dread to say!   3060
He shall be deemed as I see fit,   have no doubt of that.'

Then he sent out signals   to certain lords on each side
To leave off the assault   for the city had yielded.
The eldest son of the Earl   had been sent with the keys
So by lordly assent,   that same night, fighting ceased.   3065
The Duke is sent to Dover,   despatched with strong knights,
To dwell in dread sadness   and see out his days. †
Then from the furthest gate   fled folk without number,
For fear of Sir Florent   and his fierce knights;
They stream from the city   and speed to the woods   3070
With victuals and vessels   and precious vestments.
When a banner is raised   above the broad gates,
Sir Florent was never   so cheerful nor favoured!
The knight high on his hill   beheld the walls
And said, 'I see by that sign   that the city is ours!'†   3075
Arthur enters anon   with his host all arrayed
At the hour of undern,   intending to bide.
The king cried aloud   to all his divisions
That, on pain of life and limb   and of any lands held,
No loyal liegeman   who belonged to him   3080
Should lie with no lady,   nor no loyal maiden,
Nor wife of no burgess,   nor by that any woman,
Nor debase any man   who belonged to that borough.

When good King Arthur   had loyally conquered that place
And dispersed his rich kinsmen   to take hold of the castle, 3085
All its cruel, keen defenders,   by his skill at arms,
Acknowledged him king,   whether captain or constable.
    He devised and dealt   with diverse lords
A dowry for the Duchess   and her dear children;
And wardens were chosen   to wield power in those lands   3090
That he had won by war   and through his wise knights.
Thus in Lorraine he lingers,   lord in his own right,
Sets laws in that land   as he believes fit,
And on Lammas day   he wends to Lucerne,
And with equal leisure   lingers there too.   3095
There his galleys were gathered,   a full great number,
All glittering as glass   under green hills,
With cabins bedecked   as befits kings anointed;
And clear cloth of gold   cast for his knights and others;
Soon they stowed their stuff   and stabled their horses   3100
Then strike over the lake   straight towards the far strand.
Now he moves his might   with mirth in his heart
Over mountains so high,   and by marvellous ways,
Goes in by Mount Gotthard   and wins the guard tower,
Aggrieving the garrison   with grisly wounds!   3105
When he has passed the heights,   then the king halts,
Beholding about him   all his whole battalions,
And looking upon Lombardy,   he exclaims out loud:
'I think I be lord   of that likeable land!'
With anointed kings   they continue to Como;   3110
Key to that country   and all in that kingdom.
Sir Florent and Sir Floridas   then forged ahead
With over five hundred   fierce French men;
They sought quickly to gain   that city unseen
By setting an ambush,   as suited them best.   3115
Then soon around sunrise   there issues from that city
Scouts scanning on horses,   skilfully shifting;
They scour with skill   as they skip on the hills
To discover those skulking   who might cause them discomfort.
Peasants and shepherds   passed out after them[†]   3120
Through the proud gates   with pigs to the pasture;

Boys in the suburbs   laughed loud and babbled
When a brave boar   runs bold to the fields.
Then our ambush breaks out   and wins the bridge,
Bustles into that borough   with banners displayed,   3125
Stick and stab through   those who stand against them;
Four streets they destroyed   before they had stopped!

 Now the Conqueror is in Como   and holds his court
With anointed kings   within its local castle;
He counsels the commons   of that town and country   3130
With comforting talk,   all careful and knightly,
Makes one of his keen knights   its constable quickly;
Thus both country and king   were now in accord.
The Sire of Milan   heard say that city was taken,
And sent to Arthur   certain of his lords   3135
With sixty good horses   bearing great sums of gold;
He besought him as sovereign   to spare all his people,
And said he would always   be his honest subject,
With courteous obeisance   for his several lands:
For Piacenza, for Ponte   and for Pontremoli,   3140
For Pisa and for Pavia   and grandly proffers
Purple dye, palls of silk   and precious stones,
Palfreys fit for a prince   and proven steeds;
And annually, for Milan,   one million in gold,
Given meekly at Martinmas,   a treasure in homage,   3145
And always, without asking,   he and his heirs
Will show Arthur allegiance   while his life lasts.
The king, by his counsel,   grants the Sire safe conduct
So he comes to Como   to acknowledge him as lord.

 Into Tuscany he turns   when seemed the right time,   3150
And swiftly takes towns   with towers full high;
He pounds down walls   and wounded knights,
He overturns towers   and torments the people,
He wrought sorrow on widows   who lament with woe, †
Swearing oaths, weeping often   and wringing their hands;   3155
And he wastes all with war   wheresoever he rides;
Great anguish he wrought   on their wealth and their dwellings!

He pounds down walls   and wounded knights,
He overturns towers   and torments the people

Thus they spring and spread out   and spare very few,
Spitefully seize spoil   and displant every vine,
Spend without sparing,   spilling their savings,   3160
And with many spears   they speed on to Spoleto.
From Spain to Prussia   sprang word of his exploits;
Those who spoke of his spending   did so with disparagement.
This valiant king veered   his reins to Viterbo;
Advisedly in that vale   he victuals his nobles   3165
On Vernage and other wine,   and on baked venison,
And on the lands of that Viscount,   he ventures to linger.

Soon the vanguard, with vigour,   leave their saddles void
In the vale of Vertennon,   among all the vines;
There this sovereign sojourns   with sweet joy in his heart   3170
To wait and see if Senators   would send him word.
With rich wine a-plenty   and riot and revelry
Did both ruler and regal men   of the Round Table,
With much mirth and music   and many good games,
Make as merry on this earth   as no men ever did!   3175

 But on a Saturday, at noon,   some seven nights later,
The most skilled of Cardinals   which belonged to that court
Comes and kneels to the Conqueror   and speaks in this way:
He prays for peace   and profusely begs him
          To have pity on the Pope   that was under pressure   3180
And besought a truce   for the sake of the Lord
Lasting some seven days,   so they could meet in council,
Then they would certainly see him   the Sunday thereafter
In the City of Rome,   as their sovereign and lord,
And kindly crown him   by their own hands with chrism,   3185
With his sceptre and sword   as sovereign and lord.
Hostages will come   as captive security,
All excellent heirs,   some eight score in number,
In Tharsian togas,   full richly attired,
And be consigned to the king   and his comely knights.   3190
When they had settled that truce,   with trumpets blown after,
They turn into a tent   where tables were raised;
The king himself sits,   with certain lords,
All blithe on those benches   beneath a silk awning.
All the senators are sat,   alone by themselves,   3195
And solemnly served   with most splendid food.
The king with mild words,   most mighty with mirth,
Regales all the Romans   at his rich table,
Comforts the Cardinal,   himself like a knight,
And, as romance tells us,   this right regal royal   3200
Reverences the Romans   with his rich table.
When they thought it was right   those cultured, clever men
Take their leave of the king   to return again
To their city that night,   as swiftly as they could,

128

And they leave their fellow Romans   as hostage with Arthur.   3205

Then this rich royal king   proclaims with these words:
'Now may we revel and rest,   for Rome is ours!
Put our hostages at ease,   these praiseworthy innocents,
And see they are all looked after   while living as my guests.
As Emperor of Germany,   and of the East marches,†   3210
We shall be overlord of all   that live on this earth!
We will capture these lands   by the Cross-days
And so at Christmas Day   be crowned thereafter,
Reigning in all my realms   and holding my Round Table,
Free to do as I wish   with the revenues from Rome;   3215
Then go over the great seas   with good men of arms
To revenge our Christ   that died on the rood!'

Then this comely king,   as the chronicles tell,
Bounds brightly to bed   with a blithe heart;
With sleight he slackens his girdle   and slings off his clothes,   3220
And through sloth of slumber   falls into sleep.
But one hour after midnight   all his mood changed;
In that early morning   he met with a nightmare!
And when his dire dream   was drawn to an end,
The king shudders with dread,   as if he should die;   3225
He sends for his sages   and tells of his fears:
'In faith, I was never so afraid   since the day I was formed,
Therefore readily read   and interpret my visions
Which I shall, right and properly,   relate with the truth.
I dreamt I was all alone,   wandering in a wood,   3230
And I had no wit nor idea   as to which way to go,
For wolves and wild swine   and wicked beasts
Walked in those wastes   while seeking their quarry;
And lions all loathsome   licked their teeth
All from lapping the blood   of my loyal knights!   3235
Through that forest I fled,   where flowers grew high,
From my feelings of fear   of those foul things,
And emerged in a meadow,   encircled by mountains;
Men may see no merrier place   on all middle-earth!
These acres were compassed   and cast all about   3240

With clover and clerewort   cladding the ground
The vale was environed   with vines of silver,
All with grapes of gold,   none was ever greater,
With arbours about it   of all kinds of trees
Which herds grazed beneath   in those high gardens;   3245
Every fruit could be found there   which flourished on earth
On those fine fecund boughs   finely hedging those fields;
No damp raindrops fell here   that should damage them;
In the drought of the day   all the flowers were dry!

In that early morning   he met with a nightmare!
And when his dire dream   was drawn to an end,
The king shudders with dread,   as if he should die

'Then, down from the clouds   descends into that dale   3250
A duchess, dressed dearly   with a diapered design
On a surcoat of silk,   most splendidly hewed,
Lined with pelts of otter   all low down to the hems,
And with ladylike lappets,   a yard in length;
She was richly adorned   with ribbons of gold   3255
And brooches and bezants   and many bright stones
That embellished her back   and her breast everywhere.
Her caul and her coronet   were so cleanly arrayed
That such a comely complexion   could not be recalled!
She whirled with her white hands   a wheel about her,†   3260
And rotated that wheel,   as she would, with great cunning;
That round wheel was clad   with red gold and royal stones,
Arrayed with great riches   and plentiful rubies;
The spokes were all splinted   with spliced straps of silver,
And a full spear in length   spanned the space to the hub;   3265
On this was a chair,   of chalk-white silver,
Chequered with choice gems   of changing hues;
Round its arc, on the rim,   clung on kings in a row
With crowns of clear gold,   all cracked asunder:
Six from that seat   had been tossed in turn   3270
And each sire said himself   these words one by one:
"I well rue the day   that I reigned and ruled;
Though never such a rich king   did reign on earth!
When I rode in my realm,   I relished naught more
Than to hunt, ride and revel   and hold folk to ransom!   3275
And thus did I spend my days   in such deeds as these;
Therefore, most deeply,   I am truly damned!"
'The first was a little man,   fallen below,
His loins lay all lean   and most loathsome to see,
His locks grey and long,   a full yard in length,   3280
His looks and his build   now all crippled and lame;
One eye of that noble   was brighter than silver,
The other more yellow   than the yolk of an egg.
'"I was lord," said that fellow,   "of great lands a-plenty,
And all folk that lived on earth   bowed low to me;   3285
Alas, I am now unclad   with no poultice to heal me,
So it is I am lost –   as all can truly see!"

'The second, I say surely,   that spoke after him,
Seemed, to my eye, a stalwart   and stronger in arms;
Yet he sighed unsoundly,   and said these words: 3290
"On that seat have I sat,   as sovereign and lord,
And ladies all loved   to hold me in their arms;
But now my lordships are lost   and laid low for ever!"

'The third man seemed thrusting,   with shoulders thickset,
No throng could threaten him   though you might gather thirty!   3295
His diadem had slipped down;   this was daubed with stones
And indented, with diamonds,   all adorned in order.
"In my day I was dreaded,"   he said, "in diverse realms;
Now I am damned every day   till my death to be doleful."

'The fourth was a fair man,   ferocious in arms,   3300
The finest in figure   that ever was formed!
"I was a fellow of faith," he said,   "when I ruled the field,
Famed in lands afar   and a flower of all kings;
Now my face is faded,   foul deeds have become me,
For I am fallen from high   and friendless for sure!"   3305

'The fifth man was finer   than any of those fellows,
Both forceful and fierce,   with foaming lips;
He held fast on the felloes   but then his arms failed
Such that he fell freely   some fifty feet down;
Yet from this spill he sprung   and spread out his arms,   3310
And from those spear-length spokes,   he speaks these words:
"I was once Sire of Syria,   and sat high above
The sovereigns and senators   of several kingdoms;
Now from such grace   I am fallen full suddenly,
And because of my sins   that seat is denied me!"   3315

'The sixth had a psalter,   most seemly bound
With a cover of silk   and exquisitely sewn,
A harp and a hand-sling   with hard flint stones;
What harms have hurt him   he quickly halloos:
"I was deemed in my days,   by my deeds of arms   3320

One of the doughtiest   that duelled on earth;
But I was marred in my reign,   when at my most mighty,
By a mild maiden,   as moves us all." †

'Two more kings were climbing   and clawing up high;
They covet with zeal   the crest of that circle.   3325
"This chair of choice gems," they said,   "we are challenged to reach
As two of the most chiefly   chosen on earth!" †
They were chalk-white like children   in cheek and elsewhere
Yet they never achieved   that great chair above them;
The first was finely noble   with a large forehead,   3330
The fairest of face   that ever was formed,
And wore noble blue robes   blessed and embellished
With gold fleur-de-lys   flourished all over;
The other was clad   in a coat of clear silver,
With a most comely cross   created from gold,   3335
With four crafted crosslets   between each quarter limb, †
Thus I came to know that   this king was a Christian.

'Then I went to that woman,   and greet her warmly,
And she said, "A most worthy welcome!   It is well that
         you find us;
You ought to worship my will,   as you should know
         above all   3340
Of those valiant men   that ever was upon earth,
That all your warlike renown   was all won with my help;
I have been friendly, fine fellow,   and foreign to your foes,
As in faith you have found,   and your noble followers,
When I felled down Sir Frollo   with his fearsome knights;†   3345
And thus the fruits of all France   are freely yours.
You shall achieve this chair,   I choose this myself,
Above all of the chieftains   most chosen on earth."
She lifts me up lightly   with her nimble hands
And sits me softly in that seat,   replete with my sceptre;   3350
Craftily, with a comb,   she combed my hair
So its crimpled locks crisply   rolled from my crown;
Then she dressed me in a diadem,   that was finely adorned,
Proffers me a bright orb   peppered with priceless gems,

Enamelled all in azure,   the earth depicted thereon   3355
With the salt sea encircled   all severally around
As a sign I was truly   sovereign of the world. †
Then she brought me a sword   with bright burnished hilts
And bade me brandish that blade: "This broadsword is my own;
Many swiped by its sweep   have sweat all their blood   3360
And when you swing with this sword,   you will always hold sway."
Then she rises when ready,   to rest at her leisure,
In the realms of a wood   so rich and so rare
That no prince upon earth   possessed such a prime orchard;
And only in Paradise   could plants be so pleasing.   3365
She bade the boughs should bow down   and bring to my hands
The best that they bear   on their highest branches;
Which they yielded at her behest,   all wholly at once,
The highest trees in each holt,   I would have you know truly;
She bade me not to refrain   from picking fruit of my choice: 3370
"Find yourself the finest,   you fairest of nobles,
And reach for the ripest;   let yourself run riot!
Rest now, royal king   for all Rome is yours!
I shall readily roll   this round wheel to your gain
And pour for you rich wine,   served in rinsed cups!"   3375
Then she went to the well   by the edge of the wood,
That welled up with wine   and most wonderfully runs;
She caught up a cupful   and covered it fairly
Then bade me draw near   and drink a draught to herself.

'In this way she led me   about the length of an hour,   3380
With all the liking and love   that any lord should wish for;
But as mid-day drew on us,   all her mood changed,
And she made much menace   with marvellous words;
When I cried at her speaking,   she cast down her brows:
"King, you call out for nothing,   by Christ that made me!   3385
For you shall lose in this gamble   and your life after;
You have lived long enough   delighting in lordship!"
She whirls that wheel about her   and I whirl down below
Till all my four quarters   were quick-quashed to pieces,
And I was chopped all asunder,   as if chined by that chair!   3390
I have churned with chill fear   since this all chanced upon me

And to wit I have wakened   all weary from dreaming
And wish to know by your words   what woes are foretold.'

'Fair lord,' say the confidants,   'your fortunes have faded,
For you have found your true foe,   however you face her!   3395
You have reached your high point,   I hold to you truly!
Challenge her as you will,   you will achieve no more!
You have shed so much blood   and slain many sure men,
Civilians, through surquedry,   in several kingdoms;
Be now shriven for shame   and shape up for your end!†   3400
Sir King, surely reflect,   take heed of this vision,
For you shall fall fiercely   within just five winters!
Found abbeys in France,   the fruits shall be yours,
For Frollo, for Feraunt   and for their fierce knights, †
That you felled most foully   and left dead in France;   3405
Take heed too of those other kings,   think of them in your heart,
Who were likewise conquerors,   crowned so on earth:
The eldest was Alexander,   lauded all round the world;
The next, Hector of Troy,   that greatest of knights;
The third, Julius Caesar,   held by all as a giant,   3410
Justly judged by his lords   as a majestic warrior;
The fourth was Sir Judas,   a jouster most noble,
A masterful Maccabee,   the mightiest in strength;
The fifth one was Joshua,   that jolly man of arms
Who, in Jerusalem,   made his host joyous;   3415
The sixth was David, the Dauntless,   deemed among kings
One of the doughtiest   that ever was dubbed,
For he slayed with a sling,   by sleight of his hands,
That great giant Goliath,   the grimmest on earth;
And who ended his days   composing all the dear psalms   3420
Which now grace every psalter   with his splendid words.
Of those two climbing kings,   I can truthfully claim,
The first is called Charlemagne,   sire king of the Franks;
Known as cruel and keen,   and beheld as a conqueror,
He shall claim by conquest   many great countries;   3425
He shall capture the crown   that Christ bears himself,
And that bleeding lance,   that leapt to his heart
While crucified on the cross;   and the cruel cutting nails –

135

He shall claim them all back, knightly for Christians.
The other shall be Godfrey, who will avenge God,   3430
All on Good Friday with gay gallant knights;
He shall be Lord of Lorraine, by leave of his father,
And, in Jerusalem, will make much joy happen:
He shall recover the true cross by craft of arms
And then be crowned king, anointed with chrism;   3435
No other duke in his day shall see such a destiny,
Nor with such mischief be tested when the true tale is told!
Therefore fortune fetches you to fill up this number,
As one of the nine named most noble on earth;
To be read in romances by royal knights,   3440
Recalled and recounted by kings of renown,
And deemed until Doomsday for deeds in arms,
Known abroad as the doughtiest ever to duel on earth:
Countless clerics and kings will acclaim all your deeds
And keep your conquests alive in chronicles for ever!   3445
But the wolves in the wood and wild beasts in your dream
Are some wicked men that will worry your realm;
They entered in your absence to worry your people,
With alien hosts all from unknown lands.
You will receive tidings, within ten days I trust,   3450
That some torment has taken place since you turned from home;
You must recant and renounce all your rotten deeds
Or you will rapidly repent for your sorrowful work!
Man, mend your ways, or mischance will befall you,
Meekly now ask for mercy and let your soul not be damned!'   3455

Then the royal king rises and dressed in his robes:
A red aketon of roses, the richest of flowers,
A pysan, a paunce and a prized girdle;
He draws up a hood resplendent in scarlet,
 A pavise to his pillion hat, picked out most fair   3460
With prize gems of the Orient and precious stones;
His gloves are gaily gilt, engraved at the hems,
With rubies like grains in most gracious display.
With no one but himself, a broadsword and best greyhound,
He bounds over a broad mead, boiling at heart,   3465

He steps forth on a path,   stalking lonely still ways,
Then, stupefied, stops   at a high road in study:
At where rises the sun   he sees coming there,
Rushing quick towards Rome   by the readiest way,
A rider with a round cloak   and right roomy clothes,   3470
With a hat and high boots   all homely and handsome;
That fellow seemed finished   with flat farthings all over,
His skirts seemed all furnished   in shreds and all shaggy
Like scrim and in scraps,   as if festooned with scallops;
A pilgrim he appeared,   by his staff and his palm.   3475
That man greeted him graciously   and bade him good morning;
The king most lordly replied   in the language of Rome –
All in Latin, corrupted,   though politely related –
'To where do you wander,   wayfarer, alone?
While the world is at war,   great woe is at hand;   3480
There is an enemy host   under those yonder vines;
And I say, if they see you,   surely you will be sorry!
Unless from the king   you come under safe conduct
Cruel knaves will kill you   and keep what is yours –
And if you hold by the high road   they will hunt you there also – 3485
Unless you have hasty help   from his highest knights.'

Then Sir Craddock speaks   to that king himself,
'I shall forgive any my death,   so God help me –
Any grown man under God   that walks on the ground!
Let the keenest man come   who belongs to the king,   3490
   I will combat him courteously,   so Christ have my soul!
Sir you will not restrain me,   nor arrest me yourself,
For all your fine array   in the richest of raiments!
No war worries me,   I shall wend where I like,
I am in awe of no one   that is wrought upon earth!   3495
So I shall pass in my pilgrimage   on this path to Rome
To purchase my pardon   from the Pope himself;
And be purely absolved   of the pains of Purgatory.
Then I will seek safely   my sovereign lord,
Sir Arthur of England,   that admirable king!   3500
For he is in this empire,   as high men tell me,
At war in the Orient   with audacious knights!'

'Where do you come from, keen man,'　　spoke the king,
'That knows of King Arthur　　and also his knights?
Were you actually at court　　while he lived in his country?　3505
You speak so kindly of him,　　it comforts my heart!
　　Well, you have wended well,　　and wisely you seek,
And you are born of Britain,　　judging by your broad speech.' †
'I ought to know the king,　　he is my acclaimed kinsman;
I am called his companion,　　a courtly knight of his chamber!　　3510
I was called Sir Craddock,　　a knight of his great court,
Keeper of Caerleon,　　constable to the king; †
Now I am cast from my country,　　aching in my heart,
And my castle is captured　　by uncultured men.'

Then that comely king　　clasped him in his arms,　　3515
Cast off his kettle-hat　　and quickly kissed him,
And said, 'Welcome, Sir Craddock,　　as Christ must help me!
Dear cousin in kind,　　you make my blood run cold;
How fares it in Britain,　　with all my bold nobles?
Are they broken, or burned,　　or brought to their deaths?　　3520
Pray, kindly speak;　　what is the case there?
Keep no secret from me,　　I care only for truth!'

'Sire, your warden is wicked,　　and wild in his deeds;
Since you went away　　he has wrought only woe;
He has captured your castles,　　and crowned himself,　　3525
Reaping the revenues　　due to the Round Table;
He has divided the realm,　　doling honours at will;
Dubbed men from Denmark　　as dukes and earls,
Who destroyed many cities　　and split them asunder;
Upon several sides　　he has Saxons and Saracens　　3530
And has assembled a host　　under strange foreign lords:
Sovereigns of Surgenale　　with many soldiers,
Then picts and pagans,　　and well-proven knights
From Ireland and Argyle　　under men you outlawed;
All these knights are but knaves　　that belong to the mountains,　　3535
Yet lounge now in lordship　　leading all as they like;
And there, as a chieftain,　　is Sir Childrick beheld, †

That so-called chivalrous man   burdens all with sharp charges:
His men rob the religious   and rape all your nuns,
He and his greedy rabble   ride to ransom the poor;   3540
He holds all as his own   from the Humber to Hawick,
And all the Kent country   is entailed his by covenant:
Those comely castles   which belonged to the crown,
All the holts and the hoary woods   and the hard shores,
All that Hengist and Horsa   had owned in their time;[†]   3545
Seven score ships   are at sea at Southampton,
Fair full of fierce folk   that come from far-off lands
For to fight with your forces   when faced with your assault.
But naught yet of the words   which are truly the worst!
He has wedded Guinevere   and holds her as his wife,   3550
And dwells in the wild ways   of the western marches
And has wrought her with child,   as witnesses tell!
Of all of those in this world,   let woe become him,
That warden unworthy   to watch over women!
Thus has Sir Mordred   so much marred us all!   3555
So over mountains I marched   to tell you truly this much.'

Then that brilliant king   became black at heart;
With bleak bottomless woe,   all his face blanched!
'By the rood,' says the king,   'I will reap revenge!
He shall repent readily   for all his rueful works!'   3560
All weeping with woe   he went to his tents;
Without joy this wise king   awakens his nobles,
Summoned kings and others   by clarion call,
And calls them to council,   and tells them of his case:
'I am betrayed by treason,   despite all my true deeds!   3565
All my travails are tainted,   no more good shall transpire!
Torment shall betide him   who has wrought this treason,
If I take him untarnished,   as I am a true lord!
This is the man Mordred,   who I most trusted,
That has crowned himself king   and taken my castles,   3570
With the rents and the riches   of the Round Table;
He has made up his retinues   of renegade wretches
And to diverse lords   has distributed my realms,
To soldiers and Saracens   from several lands!

'But naught yet of the words   which are truly the worst!
He has wedded Guinevere   and holds her as his wife'

He has wedded Guinevere   and holds her as his wife,   3575
And if a child is achieved,   then our chances worsen!
They have embarked at sea   some seven score ships
Full of fearsome folk   to fight with my own!
Therefore to Britain the Broad   it behoves us to bustle,
To batter that baron   who has brought such bleak woe!   3580

140

Only those of my forces   with fresh mounts will fare there,
And those forged by fighting,   the flower of my knights.
I shall leave here Sir Howell,   and also Sir Hardolf,
To be lords of these lands   which belong to me here;
In Lombardy look   that there is no change of lord,   3585
And take care of all Tuscany,   attend to it as mine.
Receive all the revenues   from Rome when assessed;
Seize that city the same day   as already assigned,
Or else outside the walls   let all of the hostages
Be hanged higher than high,   all wholly at once!'   3590

 Now that bold king bounds forth   with his best knights,
And troops go with trussed gear   all travelling behind;
They turn through Tuscany,   tarrying but little,
Nor linger in Lombardy   unless the light failed;
They march over the mountains   by marvellous ways,   3595
And advance through Germany   as wins them the most time;
Through Flanders he forges   with his fierce knights,
And within fifteen days   his fleet is assembled;
He shifts on to his ships,   shunning any delay,
And shears out with a sharp wind   over the shining waters.   3600
By the rocks of his realm   he rides at anchor with ropes:
There that fleet of false men   lay afloat on the sea,
Attached chiefly together   with chains like chariots; †
And all chock-full and charged   with chivalrous knights;
Behind, on the high poop,   in helms and crests,   3605
Heathens were hidden   below all their hatchments
That were proudly portrayed   upon painted cloths,
And pinned on to each other,   a piece by a piece,
So that these rich drapes   seem doubly bedecked;
Thus these dreaded Danes   had dressed all their ships,   3610
So no dint of no dart   should do them any damage.†

Then that royal king   and ranks of the Round Table
Ready his ships for war   in red most regal;
That day he dubbed knights   and dealt out duchies,
He addresses his dromons   which draw up dragging anchors;   3615
He stuffed his top-castles   with war tools of his choosing,

141

And crossbows are bent   for their brutal use later;
Men attend to their catapults   and tension their tackle,
Broad heads of brass   were bonded to arrows; †
Gear was made ready   for those gallant garrisons;   3620
Grim goads of steel   and grapnels of iron,
And stout men-at-arms   stood in stern after stern;
Many a lovely lance   stands aloft above them,
And about the leeboards   stood lads, lords and others,
With painted shields and pavises,   pitched at each port,   3625
And behind all these hedges,   on high stood helmed knights.
Thus they were sheltered from shots   on those shining seas,
Each knight with a sheen   shone in heraldic show.
The bold king is in his barge   and rows all about,
Bareheaded for business   with beaver-hued locks;   3630
A servant bears his bright sword   and fine-beaten helm,
Which was matched with a mantlet   of silver chain mail,
And completed above   with a crown of high quality.
He coasts towards each cog   to comfort his knights:
To Clegis and Cleremond   he cries in acclaim: 3635
'Let Gawain and Galyran,   great good men, be your guides!'
To Lot and to Lionel,   he shouts out aloud,
And to Lancelot of the Lake,   these lordly words:
'Let us reclaim our country,   this coast is our own,
And make them blench bitterly,   all those bloodhounds there!   3640
Butcher them on their boats,   and burn them afterwards!
Hew them down heartily,   all those heathen hounds!
They are but half-harlot,   I will wager my hand!'

Then he comes to his own cog   and weighs the anchor,
Claims back his comely helm   with its clear mail   3645
And raises broad banners,   bedecked in noble red,
On which crowns of clear gold   are cleanly arrayed,
With a chalk-white maiden   chosen on the chief,
With a child in her arms   that is chief of all heaven:
Unchanging in that chase,   these were the chief arms†   3650
Of Arthur, the admirable,   while he lived on earth.

Then mariner and master   of ships shout and clamour
And merrily each mate   makes plans with the other;
They talk of their tactics,   how things may betide,
Haul trappings in trimly   and truss up the sails,   3655
Broaden the bonnets   and batten the hatches;
They brandish bright steel   and blow loudly on trumpets;
Standing stout on forecastles,   steering at the aft;
They strike over the straits   to where that strife will start.

Then from out of the west,   the blowing wind rises,   3660
Like a brisk, angry besom   beating sailor and sail;
She brings bashing together   the boards of those great cogs
As both bill and beam   are burst asunder:
Those forecastle bowsprits   so stoutly strike
That strakes on the starboard   are all struck to pieces!   3665
By then cog after cog,   crayers and others,
Cast grapnels across,   thrown with accurate craft:
Then were head-ropes hewn   which held up the masts;
There the combat was cruellest,   and the cracking of ships,
As great cogs from each camp   all crash asunder!   3670
Many cabins are cleaved   and cables destroyed!
Knights and keen men   came and killed brains!
Top-castles were cut down   with all their cruel weapons –
Castles most comely,   and bright coloured too!
At the mainstays thereafter   they slash and hack sideways,   3675
With each swing of the sword   so sways the mast;
And at first, from above,   fall fellows and more,
Down on folk in the forecastle;   left fallen dead!
Then they battle brutally   with bloody tackle:
Knights in their byrnies   board ships and brush boldly,   3680
Disembark from their boats   as boulders bombard them,
Yet they beat down the best   and burst every hatch;
Some great men are gored through   with iron goads,
Gaily garbed men   are gut-slimed by weapons!
Archers of England   shoot well and eagerly,   3685
And hit through the hard steel   with full hearty blows;
So wholly harmed   were those heathen knights
That despite their hard steel,   their hurt would never heal!

Then they fall to fighting,   forging forward with spears,
At the front the most fearsome   that ever have fought;   3690
And freshly each one   asks well of his fame,
Fighting wars on the water   with their foul fatal weapons.

Thus they duelled that day,   these many dubbed knights,
Till all the Danes they were dead,   and thrown into the deep!
Then the Britons with broadswords   brutally hacking,   3695
Leap up and aloft   at their lordly enemy;
And when those lords of the outlands   leap into the waters,
Then our lords all at once   laugh right out loud!
By then spars were split   and many ships spoiled
And Spaniards speedily   sprang over the side;   3700
All the keenest of their camp,   men and capable knights,
Are killed stone-cold dead   and cast overboard!
Then squires have their lives   swept swiftly away;
Heathens heaved on their hatches   as waters rose higher;
Now at once in the salt sea   some seven hundred sink!   3705
Thus what good Sir Gawain   has won by degree –
All the great cogs –   he gave to his knights,
Sir Gerin, Sir Griswold   and other great lords;
Geared with Galuth, a good friend,   he goes off beheading!
Thus all that false fleet   was despatched on the flood   3710
And so all those foreign folk   are left floating dead!

Yet that traitor on land   was stood with his tried knights
And with trumpets they trot   on steeds with their trappings,
That show under their shields   on the shining shore;
He shrinks not with shame   but shows off, high and mighty!   3715
Sir Gawain and King Arthur   then both saw advance
Some sixty thousand men   coming straight into view.
Yet the floodtide had flowed   since that fight was fought
And in pools slack and slurping,   the shore was slick quicksand
So at this low water edge   the king was loathe to land;   3720
Thus he lay out to sea   lest he lose any horses
And looked after his liegemen   and his loyal knights,
So if any were lame   they should not lose their lives.

Thus all that false fleet   was despatched on the flood
And so all those foreign folk   are left floating dead!

Then good Sir Gawain,   he takes a galley,
And glides up a narrow gulf   with good men of arms;   3725
With great anger, on grounding,   he goes into the water
Right up to his girdle   in all his gilt gear;
Then shoots up on the sand   in sight of those lords,
Just himself and a small troop,   I am sorry to say!
With banners all badged,   boasting of his arms,   3730
He bounds up on to the bank   in his bright clothes;
He bids his flag-bearer: 'Busk now, be quick,

To that broad battle   on that bank over there;
I assure you solemnly   I shall be right behind;
See you blench from no blade,   nor from no bright weapon,   3735
But bear down on their best   and bring them to their doom!
Let their boasts not browbeat you,   be the bravest on earth;
You have borne my banners   in many great battles –
We shall fell all those felons,   the Fiend take their souls!
Fight fast and with fury   and the field shall be ours;   3740
May I take that traitor,   trouble will betide him
That contrived of this treason   against my true lord!
From such engendered deeds,   truly little joy comes
As shall be judged on this day   as we all join in battle!'

Now over the sand   strides that band with speed   3745
And assails those mercenaries,   striking stout blows;
Breaching their shining shields,   they spike them sharply;
Those shining lance shafts   seemed shortened to nothing
As they dealt out deadly dents   with their spears like daggers
And on the damp dew   many men lie dead: 3750
Dukes and dubbed knights,   peers of the top dozen;
The doughtiest of Denmark   are undone for ever!
Thus our ranks in their rage   go on ripping byrnies,
And rive at the richest   with repulsive blows;
There they thrust to the earth,   in the thick of that throng,   3755
Some three hundred at once   of those most thirsty for battle!
But Gawain in sheer anger   could not gag his ire
And grips a spear from the ground   and runs to some gallant
Whose badge of gay gules   was graced by silver drops;
He gouges him at the gullet   with his grim lance   3760
So that this ground glaive   gored his neck asunder
And with that blunt blow   he brings on his death!
The King of Gotland he was,   a good man of arms.
Then all the vanguard begins   to vanish from the field,
Most verily vanquished   by our valiant nobles;   3765
Now they meet with the middle ward,   which Mordred leads!
Our men march on them,   as misfortune would have it,
For had Sir Gawain the grace   to hold the green hill,
He would have won, I would say,   true worship for ever!

But then Sir Gawain, in his wisdom,   waits for a while   3770
To wreak revenge on that wicked man   who caused this war,
Then marches on Sir Mordred   among all his nobles,
Including the Montagues   and other great lords. †
Then Sir Gawain was angry,   and with a great will
Fewters a fair spear   and attacks, spitting fury –   3775
'False-fostered offspring,   the Fiend have your bones!
Fie on you felon,   and all your false works!
You shall be dead and undone   for all your dirty deeds,
Unless I die this day,   if destiny so decides!'

 Then the whole enemy host   of outlawed nobles   3780
Encircles about   our most excellent knights
In a treacherous trick   contrived by the traitor;
He quickly directs   all the dukes of Denmark,
And Lithuanian leaders,   with legions a-plenty,
To surround all our men   with lances full keen†   3785
Of Saracen mercenaries   out of sundry lands;
Some sixty thousand   in splendid array
Assemble to circle   our seven score knights,
Now suddenly deceived,   by the salt shore. †
Then with gloom Sir Gawain   weeps with his grey eyes,   3790
Grieved that he had guided   his good men to this;
He knew they were wounded   and worn out from fighting;
And, for worry and woe,   all his wits failed.
Then sighing he said,   with streaming tears:
'We are beset by Saracens   on several sides!   3795
I sigh not for myself,   so help me, Our Lord,
But to see us so encircled   my sorrow is the greater.
Be doughty today   and those dukes shall be yours,
So for the sake of dear God   dread no weapon this day!
We shall all end this day   as excellent knights,   3800
Heirs to endless joy   with spotless angels!
Though we have unwittingly   wasted ourselves,
We shall work good and well   to the renown of Christ.
So we shall for those Saracens,   I truly assure you,
Sup with our Saviour   solemnly in heaven,   3805
In the presence of that precious   Prince above others,

With prophets and patriarchs   and most noble apostles,
Before His fine face,   He who formed us all!
Geldings yearn for us yonder!   He that yields to them,
While he be as quick   and quite equal in fighting,   3810
He shall never be saved,   nor succoured by Christ;
Satan will steal his soul   and sink with him into hell!'

Then Sir Gawain   grips his weapon grimly
And girds himself again   to attack that great battle;
He readies his rich sword,   correcting the chains,†   3815
Then shakes his shield,   shirking no longer,
Without care and worked-up,   he went forth headlong,
And wounds all those outlaws   with wrathful dents,
Such that all wells with blood   wherever he passes;
And though he were woeful,   he hardly wavers,   3820
And for the wrath of his lord,   he works to his renown!
He stabs steeds in the struggle,   and stalwart knights,
So that stern men in their stirrups   lie fully stone dead!
He rends with the rich steel,   he rips the chain mail;
Those ranks could not arrest him,   he had lost all his reason!   3825
He fell in a frenzy   from fierceness of heart,
He fights and fells any   that stand before him!
Such fortune never favoured   any fellow on earth!
Headlong he runs   into that whole battle,
And metes out cruel harm   on the heartiest that lives!   3830
Looking like a lion,   he launches through them all:
Every lord and leader   who stands on that land!
Yet for all of his woe,   Sir Gawain rarely paused
But wounds all those outlaws   with wonderful blows,
As if he wilfully wished   to be wasted himself;   3835
For his woes and wilfulness,   and with his wits failing,
He went as a wild beast   quick to the nearest;
All wallowed in blood,   wherever he went;
The fate of each warrior   warned the next what was coming!

Then he moves on to Sir Mordred   among all his knights,   3840
And met him mid-shield   and hammers him soundly;
And as that shirker shrinks back   from the sharp blade,
He shears him deep in the short ribs   by surely a hand-span!

The shaft shot and shuddered   into the shining traitor
So the blood which is shed   runs over his shanks,   3845
And showed as to burnish   his shining shin plates!
And as they shift and shove,   he crashes to the earth
When a lance with a lunge   lands slap on his shoulders;
Lolling back a furlong,   he falls loathsomely wounded.
Gawain flies on that renegade,   falls on to the ground;   3850
But his burning anger   turned good luck against him!
He draws a short, shocking knife,   all sheathed in silver,
And should have slain him   but no slit could be made;
His hand slipped and slid   aslant on the chain mail
And slyly the other   slides in from below: 3855
The traitor cuts him   with a hard-tempered knife
Through the helm and the head   and high into the brain:
And thus Sir Gawain is gone,   that good man of arms,
With no ready rescue;   how great was the sorrow!
Yes, Sir Gawain is gone,   that guide to so many   3860
From Gower to Guernsey,   and the great lords
Of Glamorgan, of Wales,   all grand, gallant knights:
Glee will gladden no more   those who glimpse this grim glory!

 King Frederick of Friesland,   in good faith thereafter,
Asks that false fellow   about our fierce knight;   3865
'Can you claim to have known   such a knight in your
        kingdom,
        Or what kin he might come from?   Speak to me truly;
What gallant was he   who bears these gay arms,
With this griffon of gold   that lies sprawled on the ground?
So help me God,   he has brought us great grief!   3870
He has gutted us of good men   and grieved us sorely!
He was the strongest who stood   that ever wore steel,
For he has stunned all our stable,   and destroyed us for ever!'
Then Sir Mordred made   this magnanimous speech:
'In truth, I must say, man,   this mortal was matchless;   3875
This was good Sir Gawain,   the greatest of all,
The most gracious and gallant   who lived under God,
None was hardier in hand,   nor happier in arms,
Nor higher in any   great hall under heaven;

The most lordly of leaders   while he was alive,   3880
He was lauded a lion   in lands far and wide;
Had you known him, Sir King,   in his kingdom and country,
For his craft and his courtesy,   all his kindly works,
His daring and doughtiness,   and his deeds of arms,
You would dwell on this sad deed   for the rest of your days!'   3885

Then tears trickled quickly   from the eyes of that traitor,
And he turns to one side,   talking no more,
To walk weeping away,   and ruing the day
That his words and his fate   caused such woeful works:
When he thought on this thing,   it cut through his heart;   3890
He rides sighing and sad   for the sake of his kinsman; †
When that renegade rider   himself remembered
The reverence and revelry   of the Round Table,
He repents with regret   all his rotten works
And rode away with his army,   remaining no longer,   3895
Restless with fear   lest our royal king arrive.

Then he decamps to Cornwall,   crying at heart,
Because of his kinsman   lain killed on the coast:
There, he tarries trembling,   waiting for tidings.
Then that traitor departed,   the Tuesday thereafter,   3900
Intending some treason   to work with a trick,
And in time by the Tamar,   he pitches his tents;
Meanwhile he commands   a messenger to ride,
With words for Guinevere   of how the world has changed
And how that comely king   had arrived at the coast,   3905
Fought with his fleet at sea   and felled many men;
He bade her fly far away   and flee with her children –
Until he by some wily way   would soon speak with her –
Away into Ireland,   and to those outer mountains,
And dwell there in the wilderness,   within those wastelands.   3910

Waiting in her York chamber,   she yearns with weeping eyes,
Gruesomely groaning   with grieving tears;
She passes out of the palace   with all her prize maidens

And by carriage to Chester   they choose the choicest way,
Dressed with dread in her heart,   as though ready for death;   3915
She carries on to Caerleon,   and there took the veil,
Asks to take the habit   in honour of Christ –
And all for falsehood and fraud,   and fear of her husband!

But when our wise king   learns that Gawain had landed,
He writhes with great woe,   and wrings his hands,   3920
And calls for boats to be launched   upon the low water,
Then lands like a lion   with his lordly knights,
Wades with water slip-slopping   a-slant at the girdle,
Swaggers up swiftly,   with his sword drawn,
Assembles his battles   and displays his banners,   3925
Bustles over the broad sands   with bitter rage,
And forges fierce to those fields   where the dead all lie fallen.
Of the men of that traitor,   on their steeds with their trappings,
A truthful account says   some ten thousand lay silent;
And on our side for certain   some seven score knights   3930
Are found surely as lifeless,   with their sovereign lord.

That king turns over courteously   each knightly corpse,
Earls of Africa   and Austrian nobles,
Those from Argyle and Orkney,   kings of the Irish,
The noblest of Norway   in a great many numbers,   3935
Dukes of Denmark also,   and their dubbed knights;
And the King of Gotland,   he in the gay arms,
Lies on the ground groaning,   and gored right through!
Our rich king keeps searching,   most rueful in heart,
To recover all the lost ranks   of the Round Table;   3940
Then he sees them in a cluster,   assembled together,
With slaughtered Saracens   strewn all about them;
And gracious Sir Gawain   in his gay arms,
Gripping the grass,   flat sprawled on the ground,
His banner brought down,   with its background of gules,   3945
His blade and his broad shield   all smeared with blood;
Never was our seemly king   so sorrowed in heart,
Nor so stunned into sadness   as he was by that sight.

He kneels down next to the corpse, caressing it closely,
Casts up his visor and quickly kisses him

 Thus gaunt and aghast, the good king looks on him,
And with grievous groans weeps great tears of anguish; 3950
He kneels down next to the corpse, caressing it closely,
Casts up his visor and quickly kisses him,
Looks on his eyelids that were locked fully shut,
His lips were like lead, and his looks were all faded!
Then that crowned king cries out loud in a bellow – 3955
'Dear kith and kinsman, I am cleft to the heart
For my renown is now worthless, and my war has ended!

Here is my hope, and my health,   and my happiness in arms!
My heart and my hardiness   all resided in him!
My counsel, my comfort,   he who kept my heart beating!   3960
Acclaimed king of all knights   that lived under Christ,
You were worthy to be king   though I bear the crown!
My wealth and renown   of this whole wondrous world
Was won through Sir Gawain,   and through his wit alone!

Alas!' said King Arthur,   'I am crushed by sorrow!   3965
I am utterly undone   and in all my own lands!
Oh, dreadful, dire death,   why do you delay?
Why draw out my distress?   You drown my heart!'
Swinging in grief,   the sweet king then swoons,
Sways and then swiftly   kisses him sweetly,   3970
Until this bold noble   had bloodied his beard,
As if he had been eating   fresh-butchered beasts;
Had not Sir Ewain come   and numerous great lords,
His bold heart would have burst   for that blow there and then!

'Be calm,' said these bold men,   'or you will make
blunders!   3975
Yes, such bottomless heartbreak   cannot be made better
But it brings no one renown   who goes wringing his hands
And weeps as a woman   and loses his wits!
Be knightly in countenance   as becomes a king,
And cut out such clamour,   for the love of Christ in heaven!'   3980
'I cannot stop,' said the bold king,   'because of his blood;
Either my brain will burst   or else my breast also!
Never did such soft sorrow   so sink all my heart,
I am so greatly saddened   since his blood is as mine!
My eyes never saw   such a sorrowful sight!   3985
On account of my sin,   he is stolen in sacrifice!' †
The king kneels down   and he cries clearly,
With a melancholy countenance,   speaking aloud:
'Oh, right royal God,   behold all this sorrow,
This regal red blood   which runs on the earth;   3990
It should be shrouded   and enshrined all in gold
For, so help me Lord,   it is spotless of sin!'

The king knelt crouching again,   with care in his heart,
And caught up the blood kindly   with his clean hands,
Cast it in a kettle-hat   and covered it safely,   3995
To carry it with his corpse   back to his home country.

 'Here I make this vow,'   the king spoke then,
'To the Messiah, and to Mary,   that mild queen of heaven,
I shall never ride hunting   nor release my hounds
To race after reindeer   that run upon earth;   4000
Nor let glide my greyhounds   nor let fly my goshawks,
Nor fell any fowl   that flies on the wing;
Nor fly falcon nor formel   handled from my fist
Nor on earth be joyous   with that jewel, the gyrfalcon;
Nor reign at my most royal,   nor hold my Round Table,   4005
Till the death of this dear one   be duly avenged!
Thus I shall dwell all despondent   while all my life lasts
Till dear God or sweet death   have done what they like!'

Then they caught up the corpse   with care in their hearts,
And conveyed it on a courser,   accompanied by the king,   4010
All the way to Winchester,   wending by the fast road,
Weary and woefully,   and with wounded knights.
The prior, with pious monks,   comes forth from that place
Pacing all in procession   to meet with the Prince,
Who committed to them   the corpse of that courteous knight.   4015
'Look that it be kept cleanly,   and cared for in this church,
And dirges sung for it   as due to the dead;
Redeem and esteem   his soul through high masses;
Let it not want for worship   nor for wax candles,
And see the body be embalmed   for all on earth to behold.   4020
If you keep this covenant,   you will claim great honour
When I come here again,   if Christ makes it so;
Be sure not to bury him   until they be brought low
That have wrought this woe   and made all this war happen.'

 Then one Sir Wicher,   a wise man of arms, says   4025
'I tell you to wend warily,   for this works the best:
Stay here in this city,   assemble your nobles
And bide with your boldest men   in this rich borough:

154

Call out from all countries   all your knights who hold castles,
Call out your great garrisons   of good men of arms,   4030
For in faith we are too few   to fight with all those
That we saw all assembled   upon the sea cliffs.'
Then, with a cruel countenance,   the king spoke these words:
'Sir knight, have no concern   nor disquiet at what comes:
Had I no man but myself,   singly under the sun,   4035
And I saw him in my sight   and set my hands on him,
Amongst all of his men   I would still maul him to death,
Before I had stirred from my stirrups   the length of half a steed!
I shall destroy him for ever,   strike him with his strongest,
And thereto I make my vow,   devoutly to Christ,   4040
And to his mother Mary,   that mild queen of heaven!
I will not sojourn soundly,   nor soften my heart,
In any city nor suburb   that is set upon earth,
Nor slumber nor sleep,   though my eyes grow slow,
Till that slayer be slaughtered,   no matter how slyly: 4045
I will pursue all those pagans   who destroyed my people,
Till they be pared back and penned in   at a place of my choosing!'
No one of the Round Table   dared refute or refuse him,
Nor pacify that prince   with pleasant words,
No loyal liegeman   dare look him in the eye,   4050
For so lordly in loss,   he looks back at his knights!

Then he draws into Dorset,   and delays no longer,
Doleful, without doubt,   and with dropping tears;
He carries on into Cornwall,   with care in his heart,
On the trail of that traitor,   he tracks full and true;   4055
And turns in by the Tamar   in search of that traitor, †
To find him in a forest,   the Friday thereafter.
The king alights on foot,   and fervently declares
To all his fine folk,   they will fight on this field! †

Now his enemy issues   from the edge of the woods   4060
With full hosts of aliens   in a horrible show!
Sir Mordred the Malebranche,   with many of his people,
Fans out of the forest   from every side,

Then that right royal king   of the Round Table
Rides on a regal steed   and arranges his men

In seven great battalions   in seemly display;
Some sixty thousand –   a startling sight –   4065
And all fighting folk   from faraway lands,
Their front finely fashioned   by the fresh strands!
And the host of Arthur?   His knights were about
In all, eighteen hundred,   as entered in the rolls;
Without mighty Christ,   this was a meeting unmatched,   4070
To melee in those lands   with that man and his multitude.
Then that right royal king   of the Round Table
Rides on a regal steed   and arranges his men,

And assembles his vanguard   for best battle advantage.
Sir Ewain and Sir Erik   and other great earls   4075
Then, with much honour,   take command of the middle ward
With Merrak and Meneduke,   mighty in arms;
Idrus and Alymer,   their admirable squires,
Are stood with Arthur   and seven score knights;
He rules the rear ward   readily thereafter,   4080
Reckoned the most robust   of all the Round Table,
And thus he forms up his forces,   and cries out afresh
To encourage his men quickly,   speaking these knightly words:
'I beseech you, sirs,   for the sake of Our Lord,
That you do well today   and dread no weapon!   4085
Fight fiercely now,   and defend yourselves,
Fell all yonder foul folk   and the field shall be ours!
That sort are just Saracens,   worthless and unsound!
Set on them savagely,   for the sake of Our Lord!
If today on this earth   we are destined to die,   4090
We shall be hoisted to heaven   before we are half cold!
Let not one of their soldiers   allay your lordly work;
Lay yonder lads low,   is how this game completes!
Take heed not of my life,   nor believe no tell-tales,
But with your bright weapons   be busy by my banners,   4095
And let their sternest guards   be my staunchest knights standing,
And hold them lordly aloft   to show where we lead;
If any rogue rips one down,   then rescue it quickly.
Work now for my renown,   as today my war ends!
Either my wealth or my woe   will unwind by your work!   4100
Let Christ in His comely crown   comfort you all,
You, the kindest of creatures   that a king ever lead!
I give you all my blessing,   with a blithe will,
And, all you bold Britons,   may true bliss be yours!'

Pipers called all together,   as Prime approached,   4105
Those prize men all prepared   to prove their prowess;
With brutal fierce breaths   men blow bragging trumpets
And comely cornets   to call those knights together,
And they join with jollity,   all these gentle warriors;
No jostling was jollier,   I judge, than that day   4110

157

When Britons boldly   brace shields on their arms,
Cross themselves by Christ   and cast lances in fewters!

Then the host of Sir Arthur   cries loud at his foe,
And in one shock of shields,   shoves forth without shirking;
They shot to the schiltrons,   with high ringing shouts,   4115
Through bright shining shields   and wounding knights surely!
Readily they ride,   those men of the Round Table,
Ripping through mail   with their hardened rich steel;
They burst through broad byrnies   and through burnished helms,
And hack heathen men down,   and hew throats asunder!   4120
Fighting with fine steel,   blood runs from those felled
Of the fiercest at the front,   ferocious no more.
Yet Heathens from Argyll   and Irish kings
Envelope our vanguard   with venomous men;
Pagans and Picts   with perilous weapons,   4125
Despoil our knights   with their spiteful spears
And hewed down the highest   with hearty blows!
Through the whole battle,   they hold great sway;
Thus fiercely they fight   on manifold sides,
So that of those bold Britons,   much blood spills forth   4130
And none dares rescue them   for all the riches on earth,
So strong was their stern foe   being strengthened by others:
The king dares not stir one step   but stood his ground;
Three striking attacks   were destroyed by his strength!

'Idrus,' cried Arthur,   'your help is needed!   4135
I see Sir Ewain beset   by many keen Saracens!
Be ready at the rescue,   array yourself quickly!
Hurry with your hardiest   to help your father!
Assault them on the side,   assist yonder lords;
Sorrow will haunt my life   lest they be soundly saved!'   4140
Earnestly Idrus   assures him thereafter:
'In faith he is my father,   I shall never forsake him,
He has fostered and fed me,   and my fair brothers,
But, so help me God,   I cannot go to him,
I cast aside all such blood ties   to serve only you;   4145
I have never, for nobody,   baulked at his bidding,

And been blithely obedient   to work at his behest!
He kindly commands me,   speaking these knightly words,
That I should loyally oblige you   and no other lord;
A command I shall keep to,   if Christ permits!   4150
He is my elder,   we shall both meet our end;
He will fall before me,   I shall follow after:
If he be destined to die   on this earth today,
Let Christ, comely crowned,   take care of his soul!'

Then that rich king roars,   with regret in his heart,   4155
Holding his hands up high   and looking to the heavens:
'Why had not dear God   destined this to be thus;
That I be deemed to die   instead of you all? †
    Such a loss I prefer   than to be a lifelong lord
Of all owned by Alexander   while he lived on earth.'   4160
Sir Ewain and Sir Erik,   these excellent lords,
Enter in on the host   and eagerly strike
At the heathens of Orkney   and Irish kings;
They gouge at the greatest   with their ground swords,
Hack at those hulks   with their hard weapons,   4165
Lay down those lords   with loathsome blows;
They shred to the haunches   shoulders bearing shields,
And mangle asunder   strong mail through the middle!
No earthly king   ever claimed such honour
As did King Arthur alone   on his dying day!   4170
Thus the drought of the day   dried all their hearts,
And drink-less, both died;   no dejection was greater!

Now our middle ward   meets, mixes and mingles
With Sir Mordred the Malebranche,   and many of his people.
He had been hiding behind,   within the holt edge;   4175
With his whole battle on the heath,   no harm could be greater!
He had seen the whole conflict   complete from the start;
What our chivalry had achieved   by chance of their arms!
He knew our folk were outfought,   and many more would fall;
And quickly he sets out   to encounter the king.   4180
But that chip of a churl   had changed his arms; †
For sure, he had switched   his engrailed saltire;

Now bearing three lions,   all of white silver,
Passant on purple   and picked out with gems,
So the king would not recognise   that cunning wretch!   4185
He had cast off his colours   on account of his cowardice;
But the comely king   was quick to know him
And spoke to Sir Cador,   these canny words:
'I see the traitor come yonder,   yearning to fight;
That lad with lions   likes himself too much!   4190
Torment shall betide him,   once I touch him,
Despite his treason and trickery,   I am the true lord!
Today my sword Caliburn   shall clash with Clarent,
To test keenness of kerf   and hardness of cut!
The finest forged steel   shall finesse the best armour!   4195
It was my dainty darling,   which I held most dear,
Kept for coronations   of anointed kings,
For days when I dubbed   both dukes and earls
When it was boldly borne   by its bright hilt;
I dared never deface it   by deeds of arms,   4200
But kept it always clean,   for my own kingly duties.
But now Clarent is unclad,   which is crowned king of swords,
So my wardrobe at Wallingford,   it would seem, is destroyed;
No one knew what was there,   but for Guinevere,
And she kept in safe-keeping   that courtly weapon,   4205
And those well-locked coffers   which belonged to the crown,
With rings and relics,   and the Regale of France, †
Which were found on Sir Frollo,   where he was felled.'

Then Sir Merrak, in melancholy,   moves on that man quickly
And with a mauling mace,   strikes him with might;   4210
He bursts asunder   the border of his bascinet
So that shining red blood   runs over his byrnie!
The noble blanches with shock,   and all his semblance changes,
Yet like a boar held at bay   he boldly strikes back!
He brings out that broadsword,   bright as any silver,   4215
That belonged to Arthur –   and once to Uther his father –
That was wont to be kept   in the wardrobe of Wallingford;
Thus that dire dog attacked   with such deadly dints
That the other withdrew in dread   and dared do no more;

For Sir Merrak was a man   much marred by age,   4220
And Sir Mordred was mighty,   and a man in his prime;
Come anyone in the compass –   call him knight or other –
Of the swing of that sword   he would sweat his lifeblood!

Our prince presses in fast,   perceiving of this,
And strikes into the struggle   by the strength of his hands;   4225
He meets with Sir Mordred,   mouthing with violence:
'Turn, untrue traitor,   your fortune retreats;
By great God, you shall die   by dint of my hands!
No warrior on earth   shall rescue or reach you!'
The king, wielding Caliburn,   knightly strikes him,   4230
Cutting off clearly   one corner of his shield,
And surely slices his shoulder,   with a gash of six inches
So that shining red blood   showed on all the chain mail!
He shudders and shakes,   and shrinks back a little,
But then sharply shoots forward   in his shining armour –   4235
The felon with that fine sword   then strikes afresh
And in a flash on the far side   cuts through the fillets, †
And through the jupon and jerkin   of gentle chain mail!
That fellow fetched him a flesh wound   some half a foot long;
That dread deed was his death blow;   no sadness would be greater 4240
If that doughty one died   unless God deemed to save him!

Yet, with Caliburn his sword,   he strikes back like a knight;
Recovering quickly,   he attacks, shield first,
And he swipes off the sword hand,   as he sweeps by;
Just an inch from the elbow,   he chopped it clean off.   4245
His foe sways on the greensward   in a falling swoon;
He had cut through the bright mail   and burnished steel vambrace
So that now hilt and hand   lie there on the heath!
Then freshly that fellow   lifts his foe from his faint,
Broaches him on the broad blade,   right to the bright hilt,   4250
So, blade-broached and trembling,   he braces himself for death.
'In faith,' said the fading king,   'I feel no sorrow
That ever such a false thief   should have such a fine end.'
When this fight was finished,   then that field was won,
And the false folk in the field   are all left to their fate!   4255

He swipes off the sword hand,   as he sweeps by

To a forest they fled,   and fell in the groves,
And fierce fighting folk   followed after them
Who hunt and hew down   all those heathen dogs,
And murder in the mountains   the knights of Sir Mordred;
No chieftain or child-knight   achieved an escape,   4260
But were chopped down in the chase,   and cheaply too!

 But then Sir Arthur finds later   the bodies of Sir Ewain,
And Erik the most admirable   and other great lords;
He lifts the corpses of Sir Cador   consumed by heartbreak,
Sir Clegis, Sir Cleremond,   these clean men of arms,   4265
Sir Lot, and Sir Lionel,   Sir Lancelot and Lowes,

Merrak and Meneduke,   that ever were mighty;
With languor in that field,   he lays them together,
Looked on their lifeless forms   and loudly cries in lament,
As a man who loathed life   and was lost to all mirth;   4270
Then as if mad he stumbles,   and all his strength fails,
Lifts his eyes high aloft   and all his look changes,
Then down he sways swiftly,   and falls in a swoon,
Clambers back on his knees   and cries full often:
'Oh, most comely crowned King,   I am left crushed by sorrow!   4275
All my lords in this land   are laid low and brought under
That You gifted and granted me   through Your own grace;
By the might of their hands   was my monarchy maintained,
Those who made me majestic   and master on earth;
In these terrible times   was this trouble reared   4280
By a traitor who took away   all these, my true lords!
Here rests the rich blood   of the Round Table,
Ripped apart for a rub-cock,   all is now in ruins!
I am alone in this house now,   helpless on this heath,
Like some woeful widow   who wants her man back!†   4285
I shall wail curses and weep,   and wring my hands,
For my wisdom and worship   that have flown away!
I take leave, at the end,   of all my great lords;
Here is the blood of the Britons,   bled from such life,
And now, in the juice of this day,   all my joy is ended.'   4290

Then all the remnants   of the Round Table rally,
And all of them ride   to their royal ruler;
Then seven score knights   quickly assemble,
In sight of their sovereign,   who was left so wounded;
Then that crowned king kneels   and cries out loudly: 4295
'I thank you God, for Your grace,   and Your good will
That gave us virtue and wisdom   to vanquish this man;
And granted us to be greater   than his grandiose lords!
You never soiled us with shame   nor tarnished us with dishonour,
But made us overlords always   above all other kings: 4300
We have no leisure time left   to look for other lords
For that loathsome lad   has lamed me sorely!
Let us go now to Glastonbury,   no more I gain here;

There we shall rest and remain,   while our wounds recover.
Let dear God be lauded   for this day and its deeds,   4305
Who has deemed us the destiny   to die in our own land.'

Then all wholly at once,   they hold to his behest
And gallop to Glastonbury,   going by the best road,
Enter the isle of Avalon   where Arthur alights,
And makes for a manor there,   for he might go no farther: 4310
A surgeon of Salerno   inspects his wounds,
And the king sees himself   that he cannot be saved,
So he soon said these words   to his closest retinue:
'Please call a confessor for me,   who carries Christ with him;
I must in haste take the housel,   no matter what happens;   4315
My blood-cousin Constantine   shall bear my crown, †
As becomes such a kinsman,   if Christ wills it so!
Nobles, you have my blessing   to bury our lords
Who by sword-blade in battle   were brought to their end;
And then be manly and march   to the children of Mordred – †   4320
They must be slain surreptitiously   and slung in the waters;
So that no more wicked weed   writhes again on this earth!
I warn you work as I bid   to preserve your renown!
I forgive every wrongdoing,   for the love of Christ in heaven!
If Guinevere fares well,   then long let her flower!'   4325

He murmurs *In manus*,   with his last earthly might, †
And thus his spirit passes,   and he speaks no more!

Then the barons of Britain,   bishops and others,
Go with grief-stricken hearts   together to Glastonbury,
To bury their bold king,   and bring him to the earth,   4330
With all the worship and wealth   as should be owed to him.
Then bells ring thoroughly,   and the Requiem sung;
They say masses and matins   with mournful delivery:
High religious men robed   in their rich copes;
Patriarchs and prelates   in precious clothes;   4335
Dukes and high lords   in their dark mourning dress;
Countesses kneeling,   clasping supplicant hands;
Lamenting ladies   looking low to the ground;

He murmurs *In manus,*   with his last earthly might,
And thus his spirit passes,   and he speaks no more!

All were bedecked in black,   abject women and others,
Who showed at the sepulchre   with sobbing tears;   4340
Such a sorrowful sight   was never seen in their time!

Thus ends King Arthur,   as authors all tell,
Of the blood of Hector,   son of the Trojan king,
And of Sir Priam, the prince,   praised on this earth;
From them the Britons   brought all their bold stock   4345
Into Britain the Great,   as the Brut bears witness.

Here lies Arthur, once king and king to be.

Here ends *Morte Arthure*, written by Robert of Thornton.
May the said R. Thornton, who wrote this, be blessed. Amen! [†]

NOTES

Manuscript reading comes from Brock. For references in full, see Some Further Reading.

- Preliminary Latin: The introductory lines translate as 'in the name of the Father, the Son and the Holy Spirit. Amen for the sake of Charity. Amen'.
- 1–25 *Now great … this story*: The poet adopts a characteristic introductory style of a storyteller. For example, the *Gest of Robyn Hode* (fifteenth century) ballad begins:
  Lythe (gather) and listin, gentilmen,
  That be of frebore (free-born) blode …
  (Dobson and Taylor)
- 29 *Uther*: Uther Pendragon, the father of King Arthur.
- 37 *Grasse*: Brock reads as *Grece* (Greece). Grasse is a small town north of Cannes, France (Benson and Taylor).
- 47 *Swynn*: *Swynne* in the manuscript, but also interpreted as 'Sluys'. Benson says that Swynn is an 'arm of the North Sea near Zeeland'. Krishna supports Sluys, recording that both names were used at that time.
- 61 *Caerleon*: i.e. South Wales has long been associated with the legends of King Arthur; its well-preserved Roman amphitheatre is often connected with the notion of the Round Table, as is alluded to here, along with other remains, by 'curious walls'. See also note to 3512.
- 65 *Conqueror*: King Arthur himself. The poet variously describes Arthur as king, conqueror or even Sir Arthur.
- 66 *Dozen Peers*: The manuscript has *dusperes* (with variations elsewhere in the poem, e.g. *dussepere*, 'Duke of the Dozen', line 2642), a

168

derivative of the French *douze pairs* or the Twelve Peers (the Paladins) of Charlemagne. The word suggests a generic high council of senior lords. In line 2029, for example, *dusseperez* is used to describe the Roman high command.

- 77 *West March*: As the king is in Carlisle, the reference may refer to the western part of the border in Scotland. See Glossary entry for 'Marches'.
- 83 *king to a king*: The stranger (Senator) treats Arthur not as a lord but as an equal; contemporary audiences would have expected due deference to the king and seen this behaviour as insulting.
- 87 *great seal*: The messenger has been sent under the seal of 'Lucius Iberius', whose name is perhaps a scribal error for Lucius Tiberius, a creation of Geoffrey of Monmouth in his *History of the Kings of Britain*, written around 1136 (Benson).
- 89 *arms*: The seal of the emperor shows his heraldic insignia as proof of the senator's credentials.
- 92 *Lammas day*: August 1. Lammas is the first of the harvest festivals when typically a gift of a loaf made from the new harvest was presented. Contemporary readers may have seen this as a metaphor for Lucius receiving his annual dues from Arthur. The public nature of the summons and its conditions reflect its legal status and explain Arthur's ultimate response.
- 151 *acting through wrath*: From a Just War perspective, Arthur advocates working legally and not through revenge, a balance which changes in the second half of the poem.
- 173 *on his right hand*: The most honoured position; sat next to the King at the high table.
- 209 *served from one cup*: Perhaps *the* cup; a chief serving cup from which the other sixty are filled from a large bowl.
- 212–13 *precious stones … no poison*: It was believed that precious stones served as protection against poison and evil. The tomb of Sir Hugh Calveley at Bunbury, Cheshire, features a circlet around the helmet encrusted with jewels for this purpose.
- 223–6 *curious meats … feeble fare*: The ironic observation of Arthur offering only poor British fare, having just described the wondrous food brought before the guests, might have been courtly behaviour observed by the poet. Alternatively, it may be poetic conceit; we see similar irony later on when Gawain describes himself to Priamus (line 2620).

- 235 *spices unsparingly*: Spices were an expensive commodity in the fourteenth century, indicating Arthur's great wealth.
- 245 *Giant's Tower*: Benson suggests this may imply a prehistoric edifice from pre-Brutus times when Britain was populated by giants. As the king is in Carlisle, the poet may also be referring to the keep, which even today looms large over the castle.
- 258 *win back renown*: This powerful speech by Sir Cador may be a contemporary reference to national decline during the reign of Richard II, 1377–1399.
- 277 *Belinus and Brennius*: Geoffrey of Monmouth cites both (inaccurately) as conquering Rome, where Brennius remained while Belinus returned as King of Britain. Baldwin here may be an alliterative inclusion.
- 282 *Constantine our kinsman*: In Geoffrey of Monmouth's book, Constantine succeeds his father Constantius as King of the Britons, who died at York. Geoffrey says that Constantius, a powerful Roman senator, had succeeded the native king Coel and married his daughter, Helen, apparently creating a legitimate British heir in his son. Historically, while Constantine was indeed proclaimed emperor following the death of his father Constantius in AD 305, it was circumstantial that this occurred in York; he was not a native Briton. Despite this, the part played by Constantine in reunifying the Roman Empire was a pivotal achievement, along with his conversion to Christianity which is suggested (though not proven) as occurring in AD 312. Not to be confused with the Constantine referred to at the end of the poem (see note to line 4316).
- 301 *Fifty thousand men*: Brock and Krishna have fifty thousand; Benson (followed by Armitage and Stone) use twenty thousand, a figure based on work by Gordon and Vinaver's interpretation of Malory's source version of the poem (see Historical Introduction).
- 320 *Ay, Ay*: This wonderful evocation of some form of Welsh accent reminds the reader of the mannerisms of Shakespeare's Fluellen in *Henry V*.
- 324 *the vanguard*: See note to line 390.
- 327 *Pontremoli*: The manuscript calls the city Pount Tremble; the translation of Pontremoli is indeed the 'trembling bridge'.
- 355–6 *Send knights … appropriate time*: Mediaeval sieges could be drawn out affairs, often resulting in starvation (and worse) for the inhabitants.

The Siege of Calais undertaken by Edward III following the Battle of Crécy in 1346, lasted for almost a year.

- 360–63 *snatch at his eagle ... riotous knights*: Standards on the battlefield, for example, the French *Oriflamme* (or golden flame), were key rallying points amid the confusion of fighting. Guarding such banners was a major honour.
- 375 *Genoese*: Although Genoese troops are mentioned here most likely for alliterative purposes, it was well known that Genoa provided mercenary troops in the Middle Ages. Genoese crossbowmen, on failing to make an impact against the English army at Crécy in 1346, were notoriously charged down by the French cavalry in a fit of contempt and rage.
- 390 *rear guard and battles*: A typical mediaeval English army was arrayed for the march in large units or 'battles', including the vanguard (the front of the army) and the reasguard. In battlefield formation, the main unit, or ward, would typically form the centre of the army, with the vanguard and rearguard to either side. At Crécy, the vanguard (commanded by his son, the Black Prince) was positioned to the right of King Edward III's main battle, with the rearguard to his left.
- 424 *river of Rhone*: While the Rhone is inserted for alliterative purposes, it was famous at that time as Avignon on the Rhone housed the Palais des Papes, the seat of the Avignon papacy during the Papal Schism, 1378–1417. In holding his Round Table here, a court for settling disputes, is Arthur asserting his power?
- 428 *mine down its walls*: Mining involved tunnelling under the walls of a city or castle, then propping up the foundations with wooden stays. Fires were then ignited causing the stays to collapse, and with them the wall above. The corner tower of the keep at Rochester was destroyed in this way during the siege of the castle by King John in 1215.
- 447 *Sandwich*: One of the Cinque (or five) Ports, Sandwich was a leading port for the departure of armies in the Middle Ages. Along with Hastings (the lead port), New Romney (later Rye), Hythe and Dover, the five enjoyed a wide range of privileges in return for providing vessels for royal service. Politics and changes in coastal geography led to the decline of a number of the Cinque Ports; Sandwich, now nearly two miles from the sea by river, was one victim.
- 447–50 *Seven days ... Watling Street*: The poet has a good knowledge of roads and geography, revealing how much of the Roman infrastructure

survived in the fourteenth century. Today, Watling Street is widely known as the Roman route which connects Richborough (Kent) with Holyhead (North Wales), although other Roman roads also carry this name for some of their length. The Romans travel via Catterick (482), a route consistent both with the speed and directness required by Arthur and with stretches of Roman road in northern Britain still referred to as Watling Street today. At sixty miles per day (478), the Romans must travel at an exhausting pace, though they hire fresh horses along the way (484). The poet reveals the distance from Carlisle to Sandwich as 420 miles (7 days x 60 miles), which is remarkably similar to travelling the same route today (370–400 miles depending on the route, and relying on motorways rather than A roads).

- 494 *rowed … on the flood*: The manuscript reads: *And fleede at the fore flude, in Flaundrez they rowede.* It is unlikely that a cog would have been rowed to Flanders, suggesting that the boatmen are rowing the vessel out beyond the breakers in order to catch the wind.

- 497 *Mount Gotthard*: The Gotthard Pass in the heart of the Swiss Alps was an important, though dangerous, route into Italy. In 1230, the chapel dedicated to Saint Gotthard of Hildesheim was consecrated there.

- 523 *nine kings:* This reference is unclear but may refer to the notables the poet describes earlier with whom Arthur consults after the arrival of the emissaries: Sir Gawain; Lord Uhtred of Turin (a curious inclusion in the group, given his apparent Italian connection), Sir Cador of Cornwall, King Angus of Scotland, the Lord of Brittany, the Welsh King, Sir Ewain Fitz Urien, Sir Lancelot and Sir Lot.

- 538–41 *He is spoken as one … renown of honour*: Here the king appears as almost puritanical, possibly alluding to the decadence of the crown under Richard II.

- 549 *ransom*: The capture and ransom of kings and high nobles was a key feature of mediaeval warfare. Charles, Duke of Orléans, was captured at the Battle of Agincourt in 1415 and did not see France again until 1440, when his ransom was finally paid.

- 551 *Be sure of your paid soldiers*: Mediaeval armies typically comprised a feudal levy of variable quality. An alternative was the paid mercenary; Brock translates the manuscript *sowdeours* as 'mercenaries'. Swiss mercenaries at La Bicocca in 1522 left the battlefield for lack of payment. This may be the origin of the pithy French aphorism, *point d'argent, point de Suisse* (no money, no Swiss).

- 572 *Ambyganye and Orcage*: Hamel suggests Albania and Arcadia respectively. The context suggests the emperor's reliance on heathen forces from exotic lands.
- 575 *Hyrcania*: A land near the Caspian Sea.
- 588 *Pamphilia*: An Asia Minor region.
- 610–16 *out comes the emperor … in towers*: The emperor appears like Satan with monsters in attendance; he is almost an Antichrist, ready to be slayed by the Christ-like Arthur. The Roman Emperor's summoning of Saracens and Sultans suggests, in a Christian reading, that his rule is illegitimate.
- 625 *Octaves of Hilary*: The Feast of St Hilary (of Poitiers) falls on 13 January; the Octave on the 20th. The Octaves of Hilary (20–26 January) were key to mediaeval English legal process and were the days appointed by the court for when the sheriff could return original writs. The four law terms were those of Hilary, Trinity, Easter and Michaelmas, with dates designated so that legal processes would not interfere with the larger religious festivals. It is notable that Arthur himself presides in this semi-legal context to assert his own rights; this may reflect an English king's role in the Hilary parliaments during this period. McKisack, referring to the Hilary parliament of 1397, tells us that the commons were forced to make an 'abject apology' to the king (Richard II) after submitting a complaint of extravagance against the royal household.
- 636 *palace of York*: Up to the reign of Edward III, parliament would meet peripatetically to suit the King; it met at York eleven times before Edward was crowned.
- 645 *Sir Mordred*: In many sources the illegitimate son of Arthur and his half-sister Morgause, wife of King Lot of Orkney. As this is not mentioned here, the readers might be expected to understand that Arthur's decision and intent here are pure. Contemporary audiences may have associated Mordred with an illegitimate Richard II (see Historical Introduction).
- 656–9 *forests … time is so right*: Hunting was a major pastime of mediaeval kings; Richard II was particularly fond of the sport. In this passage, Arthur tells Mordred to keep his forest free of outlaws, refers to the appropriate hunting season for deer and requests that Guinevere is ensured first choice of what is caught.
- 678 *crown you … as a king*: The manuscript says Arthur will crown Mordred 'as king', which means Mordred may consider himself

to be entitled to the throne. However, it is more likely that Arthur is promising that he will crown Mordred 'as *a* king' (of a land yet undecided); I have followed this convention, as do Stone and Armitage. If, however, we accept the manuscript at face value, the poet is showing his readers that Arthur is the author of his own downfall; he may also be alluding to the folly of nominating an untried junior to the role of king, in the manner of a juvenile Richard II. The fact that Arthur also nominates the impetuous Cador as successor (1944) before Mordred's treachery is realised, suggests the poet is showing that Arthur himself has a reckless side, which a good king should seek to avoid.

- 679–88 *Mordred … ready*: This passage is crucial to Arthur's eventual downfall. It highlights the position faced by many English kings in the period who left the country to fight abroad. When Richard II left for Ireland, for example, he returned to find Bolingbroke, a man whom he himself had exiled, and who had now returned to reclaim his own lands and ultimately Richard's crown.

- 724 *archers enough*: The vast majority of English armies in the Hundred Years War were comprised of well-trained archers. Skill at the bow was ingrained in English society, famously exhibited in the Statute of 1363 of Edward III, where every able-bodied man was instructed to 'learn and practise the art of shooting'. The Statute of Cambridge in 1388, reissued in 1410, commanded all such men to shoot at the butts on Sundays and feast days.

- 734 *Rough hacks … horses for war*: Armies took with them many different types of horse, the finest being the destrier or war horse. For general work, hacks (light ponies) and hackneys (an 'all purpose' horse developed in the fourteenth century) were used.

- 732–5 *tents and catapults … all the stuff*: Foreign ventures meant that armies had to be fully prepared. The Bayeux Tapestry shows Normans with prefabricated buildings and other items for the invasion. Treasure was also brought in coffers, either for payment of others (including mercenaries or as potential bribes to local lords) or for religious or regalia purposes; Henry V lost his treasure when his camp was attacked at Agincourt in 1415.

- 749 *shutter portholes*: As is now thought, it was the failure of the crew of the *Mary Rose* to shutter their portholes that led to the vessel sinking in the Solent in 1545.

- 750 *leads*: The manuscript reads: *Launchez lede apone lufe, lacchene ther depez*. This is difficult to translate and may refer to lead lines (for testing depth) being dropped once the sails are raised. Alternatively, the leads are dropped at a point near the luff of the sail, nearest that part of the ship with the deepest draft (although this would vary by design of the ship). A chance conversation in 2019 with 'Shoals' Scarr, a Suffolk sailor, suggests that the lead is dropped at the moment of 'luffing', when a vessel changes tack and is moving most slowly (permitting a more accurate assessment of the depth without the lead line drifting). The shallows off Sandwich, the Goodwin Sands in particular, are notorious for their many shipwrecks due to its shifting sandbanks; sounding would have been critical.
- 751–3 *lodestar … needle and stone*: The poet extols the sailors' skills; navigating by the North Star (lodestar) and by using a needle and stone, an early form of magnetic compass. Lodestone (a naturally magnetised magnetite) could be used to magnetise a needle for short periods so that it could be run through a cork, floated on water and in so doing would point to magnetic north.
- 808 *seven sciences*: Mediaeval learning centred on the seven liberal arts: the Trivium (grammar, logic, rhetoric) and the Quadrivium (arithmetic, astronomy, geometry and music).
- 850 *cruel death of its sons*: The male line was fundamental to a feudal society; if all male offspring are devoured by the giant, the implication here is that the fabric of feudal society is under threat.
- 860 *five realms*: This may be inserted purely for alliterative purposes. As the Templar is discussing France, the reference may be to different regions of the country, although this is not clear.
- 879 *till things betide better*: In mediaeval warfare, to conduct a raid into foreign lands meant either to besiege towns along the way or to treat with their inhabitants so that they would not become a threat to the rear of the army. Arthur's tactics initially are to avoid a fight, which would possibly endanger his campaign, and therefore to come to an agreement with the giant.
- 896 *pilgrimage*: The word is used ironically in relation to Arthur's visit to the mountain.
- 907 *best made in Basel*: The finest armour in this period was made in southern Europe; the reference to Basel may be for alliterative purposes

but reflects a knowledge of manufacture in Italy (Milan) and southern Germany.

- 911 *windings of silver*: the manuscript has *with wyndowes of sylver*. Some have translated this as eye slits although the context appears to relate to the chain mail aventail (see Glossary). I am suggesting the possibility that *wyndowes* might reflect either the notional 'weave' or 'winding' of the mail.

- 900–19 *After evensong … for war*: The description of Arthur readying himself against his foe mirrors the ritualistic preparations made by Gawain in *Sir Gawain and the Green Knight* (Smith, lines 568–639). Arthur's preparations accurately reflect the armour of the late fourteenth century, including the jewelled circlet.

- 922 *reindeer*: The manuscript has *rayne-dere*, literally, reindeer, from the Old English *hran* (from the Old Norse *hraen*). The Norse etymology might account for the use of the word by the poet despite the fact the habitat of the reindeer lies elsewhere.

- 920–32 *Then they rode … the saddest*: The alliterative poets prepared readers for mysterious or horrific events by prefacing them with natural scenes. This technique, part of the literary topos known as the *locus amoenus* – a beautiful place or Elysium – was used in contemporary poems such as *Pearl*, *The Parlement of the Thre Ages* and in *Sir Gawain and the Green Knight*. See also lines 2501–12.

- 964 *Wade … Gawain*: Wade, a well-known figure in Germanic mythology, makes his first appearance in English in the poem *Widsith*, as leader of the Hælsings. The father of Wayland (the magical master blacksmith), Wade's name is found in place names (e.g. Wade's Causey in the North York Moors). Wade is also mentioned in Chaucer's *Merchant's Tale*. Gawain's role and martial reputation in this poem is considerably greater than in *Sir Gawain and the Green Knight*, where he is renowned for his *luf-talking*.

- 997 *licence of lordship*: Mediaeval princes and lords were granted lands by kings, which could be added to or removed at will; in this instance, the giant has no such ruler.

- 1175 *mountains of Araby*: A reference from Geoffrey of Monmouth to Arthur slaying the giant Ritho on Mount Arvaius (thought to be Snowdon in North Wales). For his own reasons, the poet seems to have used some of Ritho's characteristics (e.g. the beads on his kirtle) and applied them to the Giant of Mont Saint Michel.

- 1211 *miracle of His Mother*: Mary was seen as interlocutor between the people and the will of God. Graffiti from this period carries poignant pleas for help, such as *Our Ladi Help* in the church at Anstey, Hertfordshire. At Cowlinge in Suffolk, a graffito reads: *Whenever you go by me; Whether man, woman or boy you be, Bear in mind you do not fail to say in passing Mary, hail* (Pritchard).
- 1225 *Castle Blank*: Many castles were finished in a limewash or deemed 'white' by the colour of their stone (for example, the keep of the Tower of London was known as the White Tower, either on account of the Caen stone, from which it is partially constructed, or the limewash applied to it subsequently). The location of Castle Blank is unclear; the reference to the ford in the following lines may suggest somewhere near the Blanchetaque ford, as used by Edward III to cross the Somme on his march from the Cotentin to Crécy in 1346.
- 1250 *French tongue ... by foreigners*: A fascinating insight into the fragility of nationality and the concept of language as key to cultural identity.
- 1312 *cuckoo*: The manuscript has *cuckewald* (cuckold). I have used 'cuckoo' to suggest the emperor's false occupancy of the Empire. The word for cuckoo (*gouk*) appears in the manuscript in line 927.
- 1341 *part of any hay pile*: Lucius is stating that he will destroy any income (or tithes) drawn from farms.
- 1385 *Sir Gayous*: As elsewhere in the poem, the characterisation is confusing. The poet may be referring to Sir Gayous beheaded in the camp, or to the knight killed in line 1380.
- 1419 *Peter the Senator*: Possibly a metaphor for Saint Peter, the gatekeeper, whose defeat may yield the keys to Rome.
- 1466–7 *swoops swing ... swoon*: The poet possesses a detailed understanding of the horrors of close-quarter combat. At Agincourt (1415), advancing knights became compressed as a consequence of arrows forcing them together. Keegan explains that piles of injured knights rose like a wall, with those underneath either crushed to death or killed by English archers using knives and mallets.
- 1471 *grief of that great lord*: Sir Boice as captive.
- 1488 *stab battling steeds*: The brutality of killing and maiming horses was not unusual; at Bannockburn (1314), the Scots employed caltrops, a type of iron ball with four protruding sharp spines, which were left on the ground to spike the hooves of the English horses, injuring them and bringing down their riders.

- 1556 *send them overseas … for yourself*: While prized prisoners were retained by mediaeval kings and lords, others could return home under strict guarantee of payment. After the Treaty of Brétigny (1360), Jean II of France, captured at Poitiers, was allowed to return to France to raise his ransom, leaving his son as surety in England. Chivalrously, he returned to captivity after learning his son had escaped.
- 1570 *all that which is temporal*: The king grants the knight the taxes and tithes due from secular properties and businesses in Toulouse; Church properties and rents are excluded.
- 1684 *treachery as behoves travelling men*: Sir Clegis appears to compare the Romans to fairground travellers, rather than honourable adversaries. His taunt also suggests that the Romans are nomadic, holding false title to the lands of Arthur.
- 1667–80 *of how … he claims*: The poem often references 'rents', or feudal dues, payable either to Arthur, the emperor or others. This exchange echoes that between Winner and Waster (*Wynnere and Wastoure*) where the two opponents debate state largesse versus austerity. The poet may be commenting on the cost of warfare or the damage done to the English purse by foreign ventures.
- 1689 *knighthood with certainty*: The King of Syria is saying, by the laws of chivalry, he will only fight with nobles of equal status. At Agincourt in 1415, one account (Monstralet) has Jean I, Duc d'Alençon, surrendering his sword to an equal but being cut down, unchivalrously.
- 1694–6 *arms are of ancestry … city of Troy*: Heraldry, revealing family lineage, is governed by strict rules, which are managed today in Britain by the College of Arms in London. The claim of Sir Clegis to be descended from Trojans – a key tenet of the Arthurian romances – echoes a manuscript of 1511 in the British Library (King's 395) tracing the descent of the English monarchy from Adam and Eve.
- 1744 *Sir Gawain*: Brock and Krishna follow the manuscript *Wawayne* (Gawain); Benson (1974) emends to *Bawdwyne* (Baldwin) which is revised back to Gawain in Benson and Taylor (1994). The alliteration would appear to be on the 'S' in 'Sir'.
- 1758 *carefully played notes*: Cador's army moves under the command of different trumpet notes according to instruction.
- 1811 *steeds like forged iron*: This may refer to the colour of the horses or their armour. Alternatively, the manuscript's *fferaunte* may reflect the

bravery and strength of the horses themselves. The knights form in a 'front' or line, similar to the French tactic *en haye*. English knights of the period mainly fought on foot, so Cador's formation is unusual.

- 1823 *spear for the chase*: The Libyan king uses a boar spear, and is therefore deemed unchivalrous.
- 1851 *fifty thousand:* it is a conceit of the epic nature of this poem that armies are of inordinate size and death is meted out in huge numbers. It is well known that mediaeval chroniclers themselves were prone to exaggeration, as has been revealed by Professor Anne Curry (*The Battle of Agincourt, Sources and Interpretations*). Her work reveals the discrepancies between the size of the English Army (6,000 to 100,000) and the French (60,000 to 'one and a half times' the size of the English) and shows the French dead at Agincourt to be anywhere between 1,500 and 10,000+. Even at the higher end of this scale, it can be appreciated that losses in battle were not on the vast scale employed by the *Arthur*-poet. Professor Curry's own estimates for Agincourt (*Agincourt, a New History*) suggest the English army numbered *c.*9,000 and the French *c.*12,000. She suggests the reason for the battle's position in the English national psyche rests in the fact that the bulk of the English army comprised relatively lowly archers while the French losses and prisoners accounted for a significant proportion of the French noble elite.
- 1866 *Cordewa*: Brock has *Cordewa*; Benson emends to *Cornett*, translating this as Corneto; Benson and Taylor (1994) revert to Cordewa (translated by Krishna as Cordova).
- 1943–5 *I am without issue … the son of my sister*: Honour was achieved by personally leading an army abroad (Edward III at Crécy; the Black Prince at Poitiers). If a king was without an heir, the risks to the kingdom were significant if he was captured or killed, which explains Arthur's reaction to Cador's compulsiveness about his apparent heir being killed. Curiously, it is Mordred, not Sir Cador, who was described as Arthur's 'nearest nephew' and 'nursling of old' (lines 689–90) and deemed worthy of guarding the queen.
- 1967 *Autun*: The manuscript has *Awguste*; Brock translates this as 'Augsburg'; Benson (and Stone) as Autun, the former Roman city of Augustodonum. The geography here is confusing; in line 1964, the manuscript has Arthur entering into *Sexxone*. Most translators have avoided calling this Saxony and instead move the action to Soissons,

as have I. Krishna is instructive on this, reflecting on Geoffrey of Monmouth as the geographical source for the action, and also highlighting research by William Mathews suggesting Val-Suzon, on the route to Autun, for *Sexxone*.

- 1991–2 *archers… schiltrons*: The arrangement of archers in English armies has been the subject of debate. Froissart, in his *Chronicles*, describes archers formed in what he calls 'herces' – thought to represent 'harrows' in shape (square blocks of archers) or 'hedges' in the manner of a hedgehog. Some writers (e.g. Oman and A. H. Burne) interpret this as follows: \……/ \……/ \……/ (where the dots represent knights and the obliques – the herces – archers). Bradbury instead promotes archers formed on the flanks of the front, driving an enemy towards the central knights: \………………/. The poem implies the latter formation; whether this is drawn from experience or from other sources is unclear.
- 2028–30 *drink… dancing*: The Romans are shown as decadent and complacent in their preparations, compared to Arthur's more rigorous investment of Soissons.
- 2048 *villainy at Viterbo*: See lines 320–29, where the Welsh king first refers to the Roman Emperor's acts at Pontremoli for which he seeks revenge.
- 2052–7 *bold shield … dragon*: This shield has been compared to that of the Visconti of Milan (a viper swallowing a man). The dolphin may refer to the French Dauphin; if so, it may reflect Arthur's rights to France being challenged by the Viscount. A contemporary audience may have seen in this the burgeoning of Milanese diplomacy in this period; the first wife of Giangaleazzo Visconti (Lord of Milan, 1385–95; Duke of Milan, 1395–1402), was Isabella de Valois (whose father was Jean II of France). Isabella died in 1373. See also the Historical Introduction for how references to Milan may help date the poem.
- 2044–94 *When … liked*: In this passage, the Welsh King, Sir Ewain Fitz Urien, Sir Lancelot and Sir Lot are fulfilling the vows they made to King Arthur at Carlisle (330–94).
- 2101–4 *Germans … wink*: The emperor uses German crossbowmen, evidenced by the 'quarrels', a crossbow bolt (2103). The crossbow was a feared weapon because it was powerful and could be used by relatively untrained soldiers. Its use (and that of slings and bows generally) against Christians was – ineffectually – banned in 1139 by Pope Innocent II.

- 2125–8 *Cuts him … help of our High Lord*: While seeming a prime example of the dark humour of this poem, the poet may also be implying that Arthur himself seems devoid of morality. Passages like this may suggest a Wycliffite agenda.
- 2184 *forgiven you my end*: The doctrine of the Just War forbade soldiers from killing as acts of revenge; it was better to be killed, in the manner of Christ's own sacrifice, than to take the life of another.
- 2198 *revenge this death*: From a Wycliffite perspective, Arthur behaves in an un-Christian fashion because he acts from revenge.
- 2264 *cruelly avenged*: Again, Arthur is shown diverting from morality – in this case by seeking revenge for Sir Kay by slaying all who are caught, rather than choosing to ransom them, as would be conventional.
- 2283 *crocodiles*: The manuscript has *Sekadrisses*; Brock suggests this may be a scribal error for *Cokadrisses*, etymologically similar to the Spanish *cocodrilo*. The poet may be using crocodiles as indicative of the exotic nature of Arthur's foes.
- 2295 *hunting for heathens*: It was the duty of heralds after the battle to seek noble lords lying in the field, and heraldry was crucial to their identification.
- 2305 *Each king by his colours*: Each coffin will be decorated with the heraldry of its king, broadcasting his fate to all.
- 2358 *four score winters*: Most emend to ten score winters. Krishna suggests that *fowre* in the manuscript is deliberate and that Arthur is 'not only giving the Romans the "payment" which they have demanded, but also making up for his own, much older grievance' (i.e. the tribute owed by Rome to his own ancestors).
- 2382 *knightly father*: In the romantic strand of the Arthurian legend, Sir Kay's father is Sir Ector, also the adoptive father of King Arthur himself.
- 2385 *Sir Kay*: The manuscript is confusing. Brock reads: *Gud Sir Cador at Came* (Good Sir Cador at Caen), a possible scribal error because Sir Cador features significantly later in the poem. However, in lines 2380–82, Sir Kay is described as being left in a coffin of crystal at Caen, which implies some form of visual lying in state; I have interpreted line 2385 as the subsequent burial of Kay. Edward, the Black Prince, died on 8 June 1376 but his funeral was on 2 September, nearly three months later. The manuscript also refers to Sir Bedwar (2384); I have

chosen to interpret him as a different knight to Sir Bedevere, although this is Bedwar's only appearance to this point.

- 2398 *Lorraine*: Arthur's motives are unclear. However, contemporary audiences may have seen the importance of removing an enemy state which might threaten Arthur's role as Holy Roman Emperor (see note to 3210), following the defeat of Lucius. As emperor, Arthur could not afford to have an aggressive Lorraine bordering the 'German Way' (see Historical Introduction) between England and Rome, by way of the Rhine, through Switzerland to Italy. It is at this point in the narrative where it can be argued that Arthur turns from a Just War warrior to vain, imperialistic king-aggressor sowing the seeds for his ultimate demise.

- 2433 *ride like a noble*: While surveying the walls at the Siege of Châlus-Chabrol in 1199, Richard the Lionheart was struck by a crossbow bolt shot, according to legend, by Bertran de Gourdon. Although pardoned by Richard, de Gourdon was subsequently flayed alive.

- 2437 *you on your horse*: The manuscript reads: *you or your horse*, but 'or' may be a scribal error.

- 2457 *show themselves*: The army appears to advance and display itself so the enemy can 'read' the heraldry on their horses and 'know' their enemy.

- 2474 *trap them inside*: The manuscript suggests the knights fear the drawbridge might be smashed asunder – *ffor dred of the drawe-brigge dasschede in sondre* – which makes sense only if it is deliberately destroyed by the defenders or used by them to destroy the attackers (unlikely). Many castles (e.g. Denbigh) and cities (e.g. York) had complex and powerful gatehouses which could trap assailants.

- 2492 *fruits of the earth*: Foraging was crucial to the food supply of mediaeval armies. Those travelling through France during the Hundred Years War foraged across a broad front of 15–20 miles from the main army.

- 2521–4 *shield ... bold chief*: The poet has a profound knowledge of heraldry. The shield of the knight (Sir Priamus) is described as gold with three black (sable) greyhounds wearing collars and chains of silver (typically shown as white in heraldry). The top third of the shield, the chief, features a carbuncle although it does not give the colour of chief. The word 'chief' is used twice, as a pun. This particular shield may represent the arms of a person known to the poet.

- 2577 *barbers of Britain*: Barber-surgeons conducted surgery and amputations in the absence of any trained doctors. Success could not be guaranteed although a notable patient, Götz von Berlichingen, who lost his hand at the Siege of Landshut in 1504, went on to live for many decades.
- 2597–8 *rebel to Rome ... wisely:* These lines appear contradictory; Krishna suggests the poet has been careless. The passage may mean that Priamus' father had to 'work his way up' to gain respect in Rome.
- 2601 *war fought with honour*: The manuscript reads: *And be wyrchipfulle werre, his awene* [own] *has he wonne.* Although Sir Priamus is described as a heathen, he admires honourable warfare. His mysterious nature and his request to be converted to Christianity imbue him with a supernatural purity not dissimilar to Chrétien de Troyes' Perceval.
- 2603 *Hector of Troy*: Sir Priamus claims descent from Troy, from whom the Britons also claim descent via Brutus. Comparisons to Hector were a sign of valour. On his death in 1376, the Black Prince was compared to Hector by both John of Malvern and Thomas Walsingham; the poet John Gower stated that the prince's feats even exceeded those of the great hero (Jones, *The Black Prince*).
- 2605 *Judas*: Judas Maccabaeus (Judah Maccabee), 'the Hammer', a Jewish leader who successfully fought against the Seleucids and liberated Jerusalem from their grasp (167–160 BC).
- 2620 *I do not call myself knight*: This passage reminds us of the riddle-like techniques of Anglo-Saxon poetry. Gawain plays with Priamus, suggesting he is humbler than he seems, and develops this by suggesting that Arthur eventually promoted him to Yeoman. Gawain is, of course, related to King Arthur himself, as is explained in lines 2638–9. Krishna suggests the passage may derive from Oliver's reluctance to reveal himself in the French *chanson de geste, Fierabras*.
- 2639 *Cousin*: *Cosyne* in the manuscript is probably used to show a blood relationship, as Gawain was the nephew of King Arthur.
- 2641 *rolls reveal*: Mediaeval documents were kept in long pipe-shaped rolls for storage. The English pipe rolls are still housed in London and cover, continuously, the financial governance of England for a 700-year period to 1833.
- 2664–7 *retinue ... freedom*: Under the rules of chivalry, Priamus has already surrendered to his captor. He does not wish his men to capture Gawain for, if this happens, not only will Gawain never be freed,

Priamus will also fail to be converted to Christianity.

- 2705–6 *four wells ... from Paradise*: Benson says these included the Fountain of Youth and fed the four great rivers of the known east: the Euphrates, Ganges, Nile and Tigris. The apse in the church of St Mary and St David at Kilpeck, Herefordshire contains a curious ribbed vaulting which has been interpreted as a stylised version of these rivers.
- 2709 *fish-whole*: The manuscript reads: *Be it frette on his flesche, thare siynues are entamed, þe freke schalle be fische halle with-in fowre howres.* 'Fish-whole' (possibly fit as a fish) may be a commonly used term for a healthy person or perhaps a metaphor for an unfilleted fish, and thus a creature brought back to life.
- 2711–13 *cleanses their wounds ... clean*: The water here most likely means the pure water in the phial.
- 2741–6 *You have forces ... worshipful knights*: The manuscript is unclear on who says these words; sometimes cited as Sir Priamus. Instead, I have allowed them as a continuation of Sir Florent's speech; this then explains Sir Gawain's pursuit of a different course.
- 2750 *prove ... prize-worthy*: Gawain tells his men that boasting through drink is one thing, being a knight is another.
- 2765 *Fawnell of Friesland ... Sir Feraunt*: Fawnell is Florent's horse. Stone says that Friesland was famous for its horses.
- 2858 *submit like a bride*: A truer translation would have 'woman' instead of 'bride' (*birde* – the modern English slang 'bird'). The choice of bride enables the alliteration to be maintained while still retaining the sense. It is fascinating that these words are uttered by Sir Gawain who, in the near contemporary *Sir Gawain and the Green Knight*, appears as the arch-exponent of the romantic art of *luf-talking*. His pithy words appear in sharp contrast to the devotional ideals of chivalry (as espoused in line 2866) and add further flavour to this poem's reputation for dark humour and, indeed, as an anti-romance.
- 2866 *loved by ladies*: Geoffroi de Charny, in his *Livre de Chevalerie*, speaks of knights' honour being exemplified by the admiration of women for their deeds.
- 2868 *Unwin nor Absalom*: Benson says that Unwin was a hero of the Goths and that the poet may have been referring to a lost English romance. Absalom, the third son of King David, was described in II Samuel as being perfect of every feature; Gawain is stating their

victory shall be unblemished; exalting his warriors to a state of biblical greatness.

- 2870 *saint of our master*: In lines 3648–51, Arthur's shield features the Virgin and Child; in *Sir Gawain and the Green Knight*, the hero has an impression of Mary painted on the inside of his shield for reassurance.
- 2874 *length of a field*: Possibly the length of a furrow (a furlong) in a mediaeval strip-field system; see Glossary entry on furlong).
- 2876 *Josephat*: Benson says that the Geste of the Vale of Josephat was a story from a Crusader romance called the *Fuerre de Gadres*.
- 2895 *wandering Jew*: The story of the Wandering Jew centres on the taunting of Christ by a Jewish tradesman on the way to His crucifixion. He is condemned for ever to walk the earth until the second coming of Christ.
- 2918 *Reversed it readily*: Priamus' actions are unclear here. He has already been refused permission to intervene but it seems that he has ridden to his own battle of troops (in the Saracen ranks) and has then 'reversed' his banner, i.e. changed sides, taking his loyal soldiers with him to fight for the Round Table. The phrase 'in the presence of lords' (2916), *in presens of lordes*, may mean 'with the permission of lords' – i.e. there would be no confusion over his actions and a potential denial of chivalric principles of his status as a prisoner.
- 2925–39 *soldiers … forsake their lord*: This curious passage conflates two separate obligations: feudal loyalty and financial payment. Priamus' soldiers owe fealty to him; simultaneously, he seems to serve different kings with his retinue, in effect becoming a mercenary leader. Irrespective of feudal obligation, every soldier was due payment for his work.
- 2955 *a spear for the chase*: A hunting or boar spear would not normally have been carried into battle, which may reflect Chastelayne's 'child-knight' status (2952), as an 'uneducated' fighter in the manner of Chrétien's naïve Perceval.
- 2975 *breast slot*: The manuscript has: *Sleyghly in at the slotte slyttes hyme thorowe*. In *Sir Gawain and the Green Knight* (Smith, line 1330), *slot* is used to describe the hollow running down the middle of the breast of a deer. The term derives from the Old French *esclot* (hoof print).
- 2998 *leashed and led in*: The manuscript reads: *laughte was, and lede in with our lele knyghttez*. *Laughte* is a conjugation of the verb *lacchene*, to catch. I have translated it as 'leashed'. In *Les Vigiles de Charles VII*,

by Martial d'Auvergne, which dates from the fifteenth century, an illumination depicts two prisoners being led from Agincourt with their arms lashed together (BnF, Departement des Manuscrits, MS Francais, 5054 fol. 11).

- 2999–3000 *chased … chasing*: Again the poet uses a graphic hunting metaphor, likening the booty to a great hunt where the quarry is plentiful.
- 3031 *a hundred pound holding*: A contemporary audience would see Arthur's largesse as significant for a herald.
- 3053 *ransacked*: The duchess knows that if the soldiers enter the city without restraint, the population will be subject to the worst ravages of mediaeval armies. Murder, looting and rape were far from uncommon in cases where citizens refused to surrender (see note to lines 355–6).
- 3059 *children, chaste men and chivalrous knights*: Arthur is allowing all those to go free who do not pose a danger to him. 'Chaste men' may refer to priests or those who are too old to fight. It is assumed that Arthur is suggesting that a surrendering 'chivalrous knight' is unlikely to turn on his captors.
- 3066–67 *The Duke … days*: The manuscript reads: *The Duke to Dovere es dyghte, and alle his dere knyghtez, To duelle in dawngere and dole the dayes of hys lyve.'* The first line refers to the Duke *and* his knights together being sent to Dover; the second to the Duke's life in the singular. I have chosen to translate the passage as the Duke being sent to Dover under control of some of Arthur's strongest knights.
- 3068–75 *furthest gate … city is ours*: See Notes on This Translation, Lines and line sequences.
- 3120 *Peasants and shepherds*: This passage suggests scouts and troops act as guards to peasant workers.
- 3154 *widows*: In bringing misery to widows, Arthur appears to break one of the great vows of chivalry, in contrast to the end of the Siege of Metz. In the following lines, his soldiers appear to have lost all discipline; the poet may be commenting on the importance of discipline to good kingship.
- 3210 *Emperor of Germany*: The Holy Roman Emperor, though crowned by the pope, was an elected position whose role included safeguarding the Christian Church. This moment highlights Arthur's pride and arrogance: he becomes emperor and will do so, it seems, without election and with the pope at his mercy. See Historical Introduction.

- 3260 *whirled … a wheel*: The Wheel of Fortune is usually depicted being cranked by Lady Fortune from the side, but here the wheel appears to whirled high above her head, its method of propulsion most likely by the action of people attempting to climb it, and turning it in the process. Perhaps the 'great cunning' she employs is in teasing the wheel round to dislodge those who climb it. The manuscript has *over-whelme*, which means overturn; perhaps she is spinning it too quickly?
- 3323 *mild maiden*: A reference to the biblical David and Bathsheba and an inference about the decline of Edward III under the influence of Alice Perrers.
- 3327 *two of the most chiefly chosen*: The kings are identified as Charlemagne and Godfrey de Bouillon (see next note), one of the leaders of the First Crusade. As becomes clear, their description as chalk-white children (3328) suggests they are almost saintly.
- 3335–6 *cross created from gold … crosslets*: The arms of the Kingdom of Jerusalem. Godfrey de Buoillon in fact rejected the title of King of Jerusalem and took instead the title *Advocatus* (Protector) of the Holy Sepulchre in 1099; he died in 1100. His refusal to wear a golden crown, when Christ wore only a crown of thorns, raises his status in the eyes of the poet.
- 3345 *Sir Frollo*: The poet's references to Geoffrey of Monmouth's *History of the Kings of Britain* (or possibly Wace) are borne out in this passage with its reference to Sir Frollo's death at the hands of Arthur.
- 3350–57 *sceptre … sovereign of the world*: Arthur is crowned by Lady Fortune as the Holy Roman Emperor (see note to line 3210 above).
- 3400 *shriven for shame*: Prior to death, a nobleman would ask a priest to absolve him of his sins.
- 3404 *Feraunt*: Feraunt in this line is an enemy of Arthur and not to be confused with Ferraunt in line 2421; it is not clear why Feraunt is singled out in this line compared to the many other knights slain by Arthur.
- 3508 *broad speech*: This passage is intimately observed. Arthur fumbles in Latin; the pilgrim also speaks in the same way, but the king is aware that he is British. The line suggests English was in common noble use at this time.
- 3512 *Caerleon*: See note to line 61. If Caerleon is a physical embodiment of the Round Table, indeed Camelot, an audience would understand

the particular significance of its capture to Arthur. As in Geoffrey of Monmouth, the name Camelot does not appear in the poem.

- 3537 *Sir Childrick*: Like others in the poem, Sir Childrick carries a name similar to another character, here Sir Cheldrick (line 2954), an ally of the Duke of Lorraine. Childrick (Laȝamon)/Chelric (Geoffrey of Monmouth) is named as being given by Mordred all the lands beyond the Humber. (See also next note.)
- 3545 *Hengist and Horsa*: Two pagan brothers from Saxony who appear in a number of different sources. In *The History of the Kings of Britain*, Geoffrey of Monmouth says they were invited into Britain by Vortigern and subsequently began to take control of the kingdom from their host before ultimately being destroyed (and damaging much of the kingdom and its leadership structure in the process). The reference to Kent (3542) may reflect the granting of the county to Hengist in return for Vortigern marrying his daughter, Rowena. The poet's use of Sir Childrick assumes a broader knowledge of the Arthurian canon by his audience; this, combined with the reference to Hengist and Horsa, would have carried a strong message: no king should make Arthur's mistake in trusting and inviting others to manage his kingdom.
- 3603 *chains like chariots*: The French fleet at Sluys (1340) was initially chained together. The longbow also came into play at the battle with great effect, which might explain the painted cloths being used for protection against arrows in lines 3605–11 (see note below).
- 3605–11 *high poop … damage*: The original passage is confusing. Stone and Armitage suggest decorated decks with heathens hiding below wooden hatches (*Hatches* in the manuscript, 3606), however, the heraldic term 'hatchment' – the coats of arms granted to knights and lords – decorating the cloth awnings makes more sense; in particular their use to deflect arrows by a process of doubling the cloth layers. The term hatchment today tends to refer to a funerary display of a person's heraldic achievements but a contemporary audience would have understood a hatchment to refer to the arms of the living.
- 3619 *Broad heads*: This may refer to inverted crescent-shaped arrow heads, designed for cutting ropes and lines.
- 3648–50 *chief*: The manuscript has *chief* in each of these three lines, and the poet is playing with the word, applying three different meanings: in heraldry, a chief is a band of colour at the top of a shield or banner (3648); Christ is chief of heaven (3649); the coat of arms, the

achievement, is the chief, or main, arms of Arthur (3650). Arthur's proud display of his heraldry contrasts with that of Mordred in the final battle (4181).

- 3773 *Montagues*: This may refer to Sir John Montagu, Earl of Salisbury, a prominent supporter of Richard II and whose part in the failed 'Epiphany Plot' of 1399/1400 (a rebellion against Henry IV while Richard was imprisoned but still alive), led to his capture and execution without trial in January 1400.

- 3785 *lances full keen*: I have interpreted *'launcez'* in this passage as a fighting unit in a mediaeval army, whereby the Saracens are arranged in lances, units, to surround Gawain. A 'lance' varied in composition; in Italy in the 1360s, the 'White Company' (mercenary veterans of the Hundred Years War, led most famously by Sir John Hawkwood) was formed of lances, each of which comprised two men-at-arms and a page. Mallet says the lances dismounted to fight, in the English fashion.

- 3789 *suddenly deceived*: Reminiscent of William the Conqueror at Hastings (1066) when his army feigned a retreat, drawing sections of the Saxon army down from their defensive positions.

- 3815 *correcting the chains*: The poet writes: *Radly of his riche swerde he reghttes the cheynys*. Some swords featured a retention chain between the hilt and the breastplate, as shown on the effigy of Rezzo von Bächlingen (*c*.1350) at the church of Bächlingen in Baden-Württemburg, Germany. Gawain may be adjusting the chain to remove kinks and enable greater flexibility. On the brass of Ralph de Knevyngton (*c*.1370) at St Michael's Church, Aveley, Essex, the chains are of considerable length to enable ease of fighting. The funeral achievements of Edward, the Black Prince, include a small length of chain, used to retain the battle helmet.

- 3891 *kinsman*: in Malory, Gawain and Mordred are half-brothers; their mother is Morgause, wife of King Lot.

- 3986 *my sin*: If the poem is allegorical, the poet may be asking his readers to reflect on the sin of pride ('surquedry') as the downfall of monarchs. Alternatively, Arthur may be suggesting that his 'sin' was not to land at low tide (and therefore causing Gawain's death).

- 4056 *Tamar*: Krishna questions the common assumption that the manuscript's *Treyntis* is a misspelling of the Tamar and instead posits the Trent, or Piddle, at Wareham (Dorset). Certainly, this would account for Arthur's army finding Mordred on 'the Friday thereafter' which suggests some time later. Tamar is retained here in order to maintain the locale of the action rather than distract the reader into thinking Arthur is in Nottinghamshire.

- 4059 *fight on this field*: Arthur's numerical disadvantage suggests that the careful choice of battleground was critical to success. His actions reflect those of Edward III at Crécy (1346), the Black Prince at Poitiers (1356) and Henry V at Agincourt (1415). In each instance, the English king – with a smaller army – selected the right ground for his troops to achieve victory, ground assessed by prior planning.
- 4158 *die instead of you all*: In comparing himself almost to Christ, Arthur is shown, perhaps, as overblown in his pride.
- 4181 *changed his arms*: Mordred deceives Arthur by changing his heraldic bearings from an engrailed saltire (a cross in the manner of St Andrew but with scalloping on its arms) to that of silver lions on purple. Mordred replicates here the lions of England, except that silver is secondary to gold in heraldic metals. Contemporaries would have equated this to Mordred being inferior to Arthur. Krishna suggests the manuscript's *churles chekyn* is more accurately translated as 'chick of a churl', and intended to be disparaging, in the manner of dog-son (line 1072), or a runt. I have used 'chip' to suggest an insignificant chip off some old (corrupt) block.
- 4207 *Regale of France*: The 'Regale' of France was a jewel presented by a king of France at the shrine of Thomas à Becket (Krishna).
- 4237 *fillets*: The manuscript has *ffelettes* (*The ffelettes of the fferrere syde he flassches in sondyre*), which Brock translates as 'fillets' and Stone and Armitage as 'rib-plates'. The word may relate to metal plates contained within the jupon or the joint between breast plate and back plate, connected or filleted in the manner of a fillet, a band or ribbon for tying the hair.
- 4285 *widow*: In this powerful exclamation we are reminded of Arthur's meeting with the widow on Mont Saint Michel (950) and the women his own army widowed (3154) during his transition from Just War monarch to a king driven by vanity and revenge.
- 4316 *Constantine*: In Geoffrey of Monmouth, Constantine succeeds Arthur and is the son of Cador of Cornwall.
- 4320 *children of Mordred*: As Arthur has no children of his own, he is pragmatic in ensuring that Mordred's children by Guinevere fail to compete with his own named successor, Constantine. Given that no

other version of the story features Mordred's potential heirs, is the poet absolving Henry IV of the murder of Richard II?

- 4326 *In manus*: *In manus tuas Domine, commendo spiritum meo* ('Into your hands, Lord, I commend my spirit), the last words of Christ (Luke 23:46).
- 4347–9 *Here lies … Amen!*: These claims must not be confused with the original authorship of the poem (see Historical Introduction). The first comes from a thirteenth-century inscription on Arthur's 'tomb'; the last was added later in the fifteenth century (Benson).

GLOSSARY

Other glossed words in a definition are in bold. For references, see Some Further Reading.

Ailette A small protective plate made of metal or hardened leather, sometimes featuring a knight's coat of arms, and worn at the shoulders to protect the neck from slashing movements. Obsolescent by the early fifteenth century. *The Luttrell Psalter* (*c*.1320-40) features an image of Sir Geoffrey Luttrell wearing ailettes; the depiction of St George in a fifteenth-century wall painting at St Cadoc's Church, Llancarfan, also shows ailettes although by then they would long have been out of fashion in warfare.

Aketon A padded jacket, sometimes referred to as a 'gambeson', to absorb blows. The term is rarely used consistently; it may be more accurate to describe it as a padded jacket worn below armour, whereas a gambeson could be worn in its own right, usually by infantry.

Anelace A type of dagger, with sharp edges on both sides, growing narrower along its length from the hilt to the point.

Arbalester A crossbowman; an 'arbalest' is a type of crossbow.

Aventail An adornment of chain mail attached to a **bascinet**, protecting the neck and upper shoulders.

Bachelor A knight who serves under a **banneret**. Knighthood in mediaeval society was a fluid status, applying to people of many different ranks.

Banneret A knight with sufficient status to command his own troops with his own banner.

Barrow In pig husbandry, a castrated male.

Barbican An outer defensive enclosure to protect the gatehouse of a castle (e.g. the magnficient barbican at Helmsley in the North Riding of Yorkshire)

192

or a city (e.g. that at Walmgate Bar, York, the only example in England of a barbican on a city wall).

Bascinet A light, open-faced helmet, which by the 1350s was also in visored form.

Battle A unit of a mediaeval army. See **ward** below.

Bezant In heraldry, coloured roundels forming part of a knight's coat of arms. Derived from the bezant, or besant, a gold Byzantian coin. Their use by the poet may simply be descriptive of circles of gold.

Bill The poet uses *bilynge* (3663). This may refer to the beak, beak head or fore peak of the ship or possibly the bowsprit.

Bonnets A part of a sail. Brock cites Falconer's *Marine Dictionary*, which states: 'Bonnet (*bonnette*, Fr.), an additional part made to fasten with latchings to the foot of the sails of small vessels with one mast in moderate winds … They are commonly one-third of the depth of the sails they belong to.'

Bracer A wrist guard used by archers to avoid the bowstring catching the flesh and bruising it. Typically made from *cuir boullie* (boiled leather), where leather was either boiled or soaked, and then hardened with glue or by the addition of metal plates The poet is fairly free with its use; few – if any – knights would have worn a bracer. In use by a knight, the poet may mean the **vambrace**.

Butler A mediaeval great hall typically featured a dais at one end, where the lord sat. At the opposite end was a buttery (for wine and beer) and a pantry (bread and general food). The role of butler, keeper of the buttery, was a great honour.

Byrnie A shirt of mail from chest to groin. By the fourteenth century, it had become a vestigial **hauberk**. Above it would be a padded **jupon**, sometimes bearing the heraldic devices of the owner.

Caliburn Excalibur, King Arthur's sword.

Caul The poet's word *kell* (3258), most likely a fine braided headdress, not unlike netting, fashioned with jewels.

Chief Heraldic term for an area/band of colour at the top of a shield or banner.

Child-knight A squire, or an untrained knight or servant.

Chimneys The Middle English *chimpnees* (168) translates more accurately as a fireplace, although most castle chambers by the fourteenth century would have had integral fireplaces with chimneys. The Romans are therefore given the greatest hospitality.

Chrism A holy, scented oil for anointing Christians at baptism. It is also used in ceremonial blessings during the coronation process; Queen Elizabeth II was herself anointed with holy oil at her coronation in 1953, hidden beneath a golden canopy held by four garter knights.

Clarent A prized ritualistic sword used by King Arthur which Guinevere gives to Mordred, in effect granting him the keys to the kingdom. It is an ironic, yet powerful, element of the poem that Arthur's fatal wound is inflicted by what is, in effect, his own sword of state.

Clerewort Thought to be a small type of clover (Brock).

Clough A crag or cliff, or (plural) an area of the same. The term is used in the poem *Adam Bell, Clim of the Clough and William of Cloudesley,* the earliest fragments of which date to 1536 although its origins date at least to the fifteenth century.

Cog A square-rigged mediaeval trading vessel, clinker built, 50–80 feet in length and capable of carrying up to 200 tons. The Bremen cog, in the German maritime museum at Bremerhaven, is roughly contemporary with the poem, dating to around 1380; it is approximately 75 feet long, and estimates suggest it could bear a cargo of approximately 130 tons.

Coneys Rabbits.

Constable A governor of a castle held in the King's name, with the responsibility to ensure the castle was kept in good order and could be defended.

Corn-bote A 'bote' was a form of payment or fine, possibly a levy on oxen by a count of their horns (Latin *cornus*), or (Krishna) exacting payment for corn when the price is at its highest, and so paying dearly for something. It is seen in context, judging by Cador's contempt, as due reward indeed (1786). Its inclusion here has been suggested as a reference to Sir Cador coming from Cornwall and is intended as a pun (Stone).

Couchant In heraldry, a creature (e.g. leopard or dog) lying with its head raised.

Couter Plate armour for the elbow. Initially relatively simple metal plating, the couter was to develop into a sophisticated, articulated protection for the entire joint.

Crayer A light trading vessel of 20–50 tons. Both the crayer and the **cog** carried a single large sail which, as the poet describes, crossed the mast when raised.

Cross-days Benson says: 'Cross-days equated to the Rogation days, three special days of prayer preceding Ascension Day (forty days after Easter).' These three rogations, known as minor rogations, occurred on the Monday, Tuesday and Wednesday, preceding Ascension Thursday in the Christian calendar.

Cupboard A table, or sideboard, for the display of the King's goblets (cups).

Diapered Diaper work (3251) relates to a series of geometric diamond-shape patterns; still used today in brickwork.

Dolphin The Dauphin. It is unclear whether the poet is referring to the Dauphin of France. Given the location of the siege and the loyalty of French lords to Arthur, this particular dauphin may be the eldest son of the Duke (see note to lines 2052–7).

Dromon A type of Byzantine rowing galley, used up to the twelfth century; the poet has *dromowndes* (3615), most likely for alliterative reasons rather than describing Arthur's actual vessels.

Elfaydes Brock uses this word (2288), which he cannot translate; Benson has *Olfendes*, which he translates as 'camels'. As the poet has already listed camels and dromedaries (2283, 2286) in his collection of exotic beasts, I have retained Brock's reading.

Engrailed In heraldry, the edge of a cross or a band when indented along all its external sides with a series of shallow parabolic concave incisions, similar to bites along the entire length.

Epiphany January 6, in Christian tradition celebrating the visit of the Magi and the manifestation of God in the Christ child.

Farthing An old English coin worth a quarter (fourth) of a penny. Its use by the poet to describe the decoration of Sir Craddock may be to indicate low value circular decorations, in contrast to the golden bezants which decorate Lady Fortune. Krishna states that no evidence has been found to suggest that the manuscript word *ferthynges* has any other meaning than that of a coin.

Fathom A measurement of six feet (see also Measurements below). On line 1103 the giant, at five fathoms, is thirty feet tall and so is five times the size of Arthur. In maritime tradition, a sailor can only be buried at sea in depths of six fathoms or more. The poet's use of the fathom as a measure of height might reflect this, indicating a connection with death and further embellishing his horror to a contemporary audience.

Felloe In the craft of the wheelwright, the outer perimeter of an open wooden wheel is typically made from a number of curved sections, or felloes. These are then joined and fully bound together and clamped to the spokes by the application of a heated iron tyre which is shrunk to fit the felloes by dint of being quenched in cold water.

Fewter A lance rest formed either as part of the saddle or a hook of metal fashioned on to the breastplate and designed to carry a heavy jousting lance. If the latter, the reference may help date the poem to early fifteenth century when metal fewters began to appear.

Fillet This may relate to metal plates stitched within the **jupon**. See also note to 4237.

Formel An archaic term for a female falcon. The poet uses *formaylle* for alliterative reasons (4003), and 'falcon' rather than 'tercel' for the male.

Frumenty A dish, popular in mediaeval Europe, made from boiled cracked wheat and sometimes with other ingredients, to accompany meat or fish.

Furlong An English measure of one eighth of a mile (220 yards or 660 feet). See also Measurements (below).

Gadlings The manuscript reads *graynez and gobelets* (913); the former is unclear, and Brock thinks the latter are 'glove ornaments'. A gadling is a small decoration on the knuckle joints of a gauntlet; if a *gobelet* is indeed a gadling, then *grayne* may be a misspelling of *groyn*, the pointed snout of a pig, i.e. pointed decorations of the gadlings; compare with line 2443 where gadlings translates as points or barbs. Its use on line 2854 reflects the manuscript's *gadelynges*, (rascals or rogues) and which I have retained to suggest Gawain's contempt of his enemies, akin to the modern slang, 'prick'.

Galuth The sword of Sir Gawain.

Genitor A form of light cavalry used particularly by the armies of Spain. Contamine says they were 'light, mobile horsemen, mounted on thoroughbreds *jinetes*, using a short stirrup, low saddles and specially shaped bits, different from those of knights in the rest of Europe, who sat on high saddles and had the advantage of a very solid seat'.

Glaive A type of polearm. The term is often used loosely to describe a range of weapons although a typical glaive would feature a long blade, up to two feet in length, mounted on the end of a shaft of wood. The rear of a glaive blade may feature additional hooks or other embellishments.

Gorget A protective plate of metal to protect the throat; this would date the writing of the poem to the fifteenth century. But if it was written in the fourteenth century, the manuscript reading *gorgere* (1772) may refer to the part of the **aventail** connected to a **bascinet**.

Gules Heraldic term for red.

Gumbald Brock translates as 'dainties'; others (e.g. Benson) as a type of meat pie.

Gyronny Heraldic term in which a shield is quartered and then again, as if dissected by a saltire. The resultant form is of eight triangles which meet at a point in the centre; the triangles will be of alternate colours (e.g. four blue, four white).

Hauberk A long metal coat of mail, as featured on the Bayeux Tapestry. The word seems to have become a generic term in Middle English for a mail shirt.

Hobby/Hobbies A small falcon, *Falco subbuteo*; the size of a kestrel.

Holt Woodland or copse, sometimes a wooded hill. From the Old English / Norse *holt* and the Old High German *holz*.

Housel The act of administering or receiving the Eucharist, consecrated Host or Sacrament, which must be taken after confession. Etymology stems from Old Norse *husl*, or Old English *husel*.

Jazerant Derived from the Italian *ghiazerino*, a protective coat made of overlapping, possibly coloured, plates, riveted to a canvas shirt. Other descriptions suggest a garment of Middle Eastern origin, typically a coat of mail, sandwiched between leather or cloth.

Jerodine Benson suggests this is a type of cloth, akin to gaberdine.

Jupon A tight-fitting over-covering, which may also have carried a knight's heraldic devices (as in *Sir Gawain and the Green Knight*); the 'jagged' edges (905) refer to a stylistic **scalloping** which was popular during this period.

Kennet A small hunting dog.

Kerf The groove made by a blade; typically used in carpentry to describe the area cut away by a saw as it proceeds through the block. A 'keener' kerf (4194), defined by the setting of the teeth, will deliver an easier cut, so a good sword would deliver a kerf designed to allow maximum momentum of the blade through the body.

Kettle-hat A primitive helmet usually worn by foot soldiers, similar in shape to the standard British infantry helmet of the two World Wars. Possibly made from leather and metal straps.

Lammas day August 1, the first of the harvest festivals. See also note to line 92.

Lappets A loosely hanging flap of material. Contemporary dress featured women's sleeves that opened out from the elbow to the wrist into an enormous cuff, perhaps 2–3 feet in length. The tomb of John de la Pole at

Chrishall, Essex (d.1379) features lappets on his wife Joan's clothes.

Lee board A large, retractable board, similar to a centre board on a modern yacht, attached to the leeward side of a vessel, and lowered to stop a sailing boat tipping over when the wind catches the sail.

Liegeman Within feudal society, a vassal who owed service or allegiance to a lord.

Mantlet (1) An additional throat guard (3632); (2) in siege warfare, also a mobile shield; both have a protective function.

Marches (also West Marches) On line 334, the Marches (more commonly the Welsh Marches) constitute the border between England and Wales, although this is a fluid construct. The word derives from the Old English *mearc* or the Norman *marka*, meaning edge or border land. In the Middle Ages, the Marches extended to the south-west of Wales (hence the Welsh 'king' referring to the 'West Marches', 334). The rest of Wales, certainly up until the conquest of Wales by Edward I, was known as *pura Wallia* (in essence, real Wales); the remainder of the country was designated the March of Wales or *Wallia marchia*. The Welsh king's reference to Welsh-land may refer to *pura Wallia*; so his army comprises true Welsh knights and knights from the Marches. See also note to line 77.

Martinmas The feast of St Martin, November 11.

Middle-earth Earth: the place between heaven and hell, the centre of the universe. From the German, *middangeard*, or middle yard (or ground).

Nine Worthies In the mediaeval period, aspirants to chivalric status looked to these figures as exemplars of martial prowess, glory and honour. Introduced in the *Voeux du Paon* of c.1310, they included three pagans (Hector, Alexander the Great, Julius Caesar); three Jews (Joshua, David, Judas Maccabeus); and three Christians (King Arthur, Charlemagne and Godfrey de Bouillon).

Occident The lands, countries or kingdoms of the West; in this case, Europe.

Paled A pale is vertical division of the shield with different colours on either side, described as 'per pale'. The poet says the shield is purple (heraldic *purpure*), paled with silver (1375); he may be suggesting what is technically a 'paly', a series of vertical stripes of the two colours.

Paunce Plate armour for the lower torso or paunch.

Pavise/Pavisers A large shield for the protection of crossbowmen (see shield bearers). The manuscript at line 2831 suggests that the pavises were carried by individual **shield bearers**; however, contemporary illuminations show crossbowmen carried their own pavises on their backs. At

Crécy (1346) and Agincourt (1415), such bowmen, *gens de trait* (generically, missile-men), formed in front of the main battle (unit of knights, e.g. the vanguard; see note to line 375).

Pillion hat Brock says this was typically worn by Doctors of Theology. The manuscript is confusing, *a pavys pillione hatt* (3460), which suggests a particular style of hat. My reading is that the 'hood' (3459) acts as a **pavise** to the hat, although most translators omit the phrase altogether. The term may be generic for a hood being used for riding purposes.

Prester John A legendary Christian patriarch and king said to rule over a faraway Eastern Christian land, Prester John was well known in the mediaeval period. In the *Travels* of the putative Sir John Mandeville (*c.*1356–7) he is also referred to as the Emperor of India. A 1455 treatise on heraldry by Richard Strangeways in the British Library (Harley, MS 2259, f. 147r) refers to the heraldic emblem of Prester John as depicting the crucifixion of Christ, a device repeated, on a blue background, in a fifteenth-century manuscript also in the same collection (Egerton, MS 3030, f. 9v). The story of Prester John is much older; Harley, MS 3099, ff. 166r–167v contains a (fictitious) letter from him to the Emperors Manuel Comnenus (1143–80) and Frederick I (1152–90).

Prime Six o'clock, the first 'hour' in the Liturgical Hours. Typically day break; the hour could vary depending on the time of year. See **undern** below.

Pysan In plate armour, another name for the **gorget** (see above). From the Old French *pizanne* or *pisanne*, the use of this may help to date the poem to the early 1400s.

Rent Feudal dues; tax revenue. See notes to line 1667–80.

Rerebrace Plate armour protecting the upper arm above the elbow.

Rood The holy cross; in church architecture, the rood screen separates the nave of the church from the chancel where the rood is placed.

Sable (1) The fine fur of the squirrel (today used in specialist paintbrushes); (2) the heraldic term for black.

Saint Christopher's Day July 25.

Scallops Pilgrims wore lead badges usually reflecting the saint who was venerated at the site to which they were travelling. The scallop is in particular the badge of St James of Compostela in Spain, also known as St James the Greater, the first of the apostles to be martyred, and acclaimed as patron of the Spanish struggle against the Moors.

Schiltron A group of soldiers, often massed spearmen but seems to apply in this poem to most kinds of soldiers.

Sendal A fine silk material; its use in line 2299 shows the gentle reverence with which the corpses are treated.

Sheriff A royal official responsible for the peace of a given county on behalf of the king. From the Old English *scīrgerefa* or shire reeve. The role today is ceremonial, with each county having a High Sheriff, holding the post for a year.

Shield bearers Crossbowmen – *schotte-mene* in the manuscript (2467) – took much longer to load and shoot their weapons in battle than longbowmen and were vulnerable to attack. Consequently, they often fought behind a large shield (see **pavise**).

Shrimp A dragon in the manuscript: *Schrympe* (767). The description of the scales resembling shields is reminiscent of the Roman *lorica squamata*, a tunic of metal plates which were layered over each other like scales to promote greater flexibility.

Siege engines Machines for attacking castles and towns and taking various forms such as mangonels or trebuchets (types of catapult) or battering rams. They could be brought to the site in component parts and assembled there, or be built from the greenwood by skilled carpenters within the army. They were positioned so they could hit their targets while being safe from attack.

Siege tower A protected mobile platform, safer than ladders, to attack the walls of a castle or city. At the top was a drawbridge with grapples that would have been lowered down to the battlements.

Sow A moveable covered vehicle beneath which sappers could work safely at the foot of the wall (either with picks or a battering ram).

Surquedry From the Old French *surquederie*, an overweening pride. The theme is also addressed in *Sir Gawain and the Green Knight*; the alliterative poets may have felt that courtiers and other nobles placed more emphasis on display than personal discipline.

Templar The Knights Templar were a military order of Catholic knights, active *c.*1119–1312, when they were disbanded under Pope Clement V. The poet may be alluding to the wealth of the Templars (841), with a criticism of the Giant of Mont Saint Michel drawing vast sums from France.

Tharsian A rich silk of Chinese origin.

Threap To contest or argue (Lancashire dialect).

Top-castle A fighting platform on the mast of a ship, often containing bowmen; not unlike a crow's nest.

Undern Nine o'clock, the third interval or 'hour' in the Liturgical Hours, or Terce. See **Prime** (above)

Vambrace That part of a suit of armour which protects the lower arm, which I have used in line 1753 for alliterative purposes.

Vernage A type of sweet white wine.

Vernicle The Holy Vernicle featured the image of Christ's face which had been miraculously imprinted on a handkerchief that St Veronica gave to Christ to use to wipe his face on his journey to Calvary. Benson says that the cult of the Vernicle was 'especially strong in the fourteenth century; Pope John XXII granted an indulgence of ten thousand days to it'. The Vernicle itself disappeared following the sack of Rome in 1527.

Wale The topmost, and thickest of the strakes, running the length of a ship to maximise strength. As guns became prevalent on ships, it became known as the 'gunwale', irrespective of the use of artillery in the vessel. The carpentry term 'waler' describes a horizontal beam of wood employed to support a series of uprights, for example in the length of a fence.

Ward Mediaeval armies were divided conventionally into three 'battles' or 'wards', typically the vanguard (the front battle on the march), the middle, or main, ward, and the rearguard. See note to line 390.

Wardrobe The royal wardrobe was a department of state, housing royal robes and regalia.

Worm A dragon or serpent.

Welkin The sky or the heavens.

MEASUREMENTS

The following is provided to assist readers with conversion of British imperial units mentioned in the text to the metric system.

Inch 2.54 centimetres. A practical measure for day-to-day use across all purposes.

Foot Twelve inches or 30.48 centimetres. A measurement of length, depth or height.

Yard Three feet or 91.44 centimetres (0.9144 metres). In common use typically a measure of length or distance rather than height.

Fathom Two yards or six feet (1.8288 metres). A maritime measure of depth. Originally the measure was one thousandth of a Nautical Mile (6080 feet).

Furlong 220 yards or 1/8 mile (201.168 metres). A measure of length, typically for agricultural purposes and land measurement but also used in horse racing. (See **acre**.)

Mile 1760 yards or eight furlongs (1.60934 kilometres). In conventional use, a measure of distance, although can be used for height or depth.

Acre 4840 square yards (4046.856 square metres). An area of land of any shape or size provided that the size in square yards is consistent. A traditional acre is calculated as 1 furlong x 1 chain (22 yards) = 1 acre (4840 square yards).

Ton 2240 pounds or twenty hundredweight (1.016 tonnes). A unit of mass, also known as the long ton; today used in particular to measure the displacement of ships.

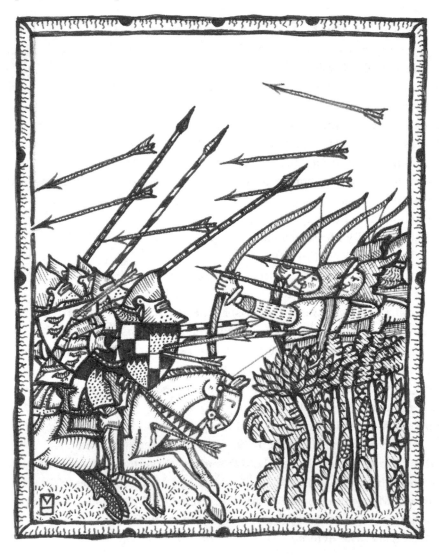

SOME FURTHER READING

Editions of the Poem

Armitage, S.: *The Death of King Arthur* (London, 2012)

Benson, L. D.: *King Arthur's Death* (Indianapolis, 1974)

Benson, L. D. and Foster, E. E.: *King Arthur's Death* (Kalamazoo, Michigan, 1994)

Brock, E.: *Morte Arthure* (Oxford, 1865)

Gardner, J.: *The Alliterative Morte Arthure, The Owl and the Nightingale and Five other Middle English Poems* (Carbondale and Edwardsville, Illinois, 1971)

Hamel, M. (ed.): *Morte Arthure: A Critical Edition* (New York, 1984)

Krishna, V.: *The Alliterative Morte Arthure, a Critical Edition* (New York, 1976)

Stone, B.: *King Arthur's Death* (Harmondsworth, 1988)

Background reading:

Andersson, T. M. and Barney, S. A.: *Contradictions: From Beowulf to Chaucer – Selected Studies of Larry D. Benson* (Aldershot and Brookfield, 1995)

Ashe, L.: *Richard II – A Brittle Glory* (Harmondsworth, 2016)

Ayton, A. and Preston, P.: *The Battle of Crécy, 1346* (Woodbridge, 2007)

Barron, W. R. J. and Weinberg, S. C.: *Laȝamon's Arthur: The Arthurian Section of Laȝamon's Brut* (Harlow, 1989)

Bellis, J. and Slater, L. (eds): *Representing War and Violence, 1250–1600* (Woodbridge, 2016)

Bennett, M.: *Agincourt, 1415 – Triumph against the Odds* (Oxford, 1991)

Bradbury, J.: *The Medieval Archer* (Woodbridge, 1985)

Burne, A. H.: *The Agincourt War* (London, 1956)

Contamine, P.: *War in the Middle Ages* (trans. M. Jones) (Oxford, 1984)

Cox, R.: *John Wyclif on War and Peace* (Woodbridge, 2014)

Curry, A.: *The Battle of Agincourt: Sources and Interpretations* (Woodbridge, 2000)

Curry, A.: *Agincourt, a New History* (Stroud, 2005)

Curry, A. (ed.): *Agincourt, 1415* (Stroud, 2000)

Curry, A. and Mercer, M.: *The Battle of Agincourt* (New Haven and London, 2015)

Davies, R. R.: *Conquest, Coexistence and Change: Wales, 1063–1415* (Oxford, 1987)

Day, M. and Steele, R. (eds): *Mum and the Sothsegger, Edited from the Manuscripts Camb. Univ. Ll.iv.14 and Brit. Mus. Add. 41666* (Oxford, 1936)

De Hamel, C. and Lovett, P.: *The Macclesfield Alphabet Book, BL Additional MS 88887* (London, 2010)

De Troyes, Chrétien: *Arthurian Romances* (trans. W. W. Kibler and C. W. Carroll) (Harmondsworth, 1991)

Delbrück, H.: *History of the Art of War, Vol. III: Medieval Warfare* (trans. W. J. Renfroe Jr) (Lincoln, Nebraska, and London, 1982)

Dobson, R. B. and Taylor, J.: *Rymes of Robyn Hood* (Oxford, 1976)

Fein, S. and Johnstone, M. (eds): *Robert Thornton and his Books: Essays on the Lincoln and London Thornton Manuscripts* (Woodbridge, 2014)

Field, P. J. C.: 'Morte Arthure, the Montagus and Milan', *Medium Ævum*, Vol. 78, No. 1 (2009), pp.98–117

Froissart, Jean: *Chronicles* (trans. G. Brereton) (Harmondsworth, 1969)

Göller, K. H. (ed.): *The Alliterative Morte Arthure: A Reassessment of the Poem* (Cambridge, 1981)

Gordon, D. et al.: *The Wilton Diptych* (London, 2015)

Gordon, E. V, and Vinaver, E.: 'New Light on the Text of the Alliterative Morte Arthure', *Medium Ævum*, Vol 6. No. 2, (1937), pp.81–98

Guenée, B.: *States and Rulers in Later Medieval Europe* (trans. J. Vale) (Oxford, 1985)

Hardy, R.: *Longbow: A Social and Military History* (Sparkford, 1976)

Heymann, F. G.: *John Žižka and the Hussite Revolution* (New York, 1955)

Howard, M.: *War in European History* (Oxford, 1976)

Jones, M.: *The Black Prince* (London, 2017)

Jones, M. K.: *Agincourt, 1415* (Barnsley, 2005)

Kaeuper, R. W. (ed.) and Kennedy, E. (trans.): *A Knight's Own Book of Chivalry by Geoffroi de Charny* (Philadelphia, 2005)

Keegan, J.: *The Face of Battle: A Study of Agincourt, Waterloo and the Somme* (London, 1976)

Keen, M.: *Chivalry* (New Haven and London, 1984)

Kerby-Fulton, K., Hilmo, M. and Olson, L.: *Opening Up Middle English Manuscripts: Literary and Visual Approaches* (Ithaca, New York, and London, 2012)

Lacy, N. J. and Grimbert, J. T. (eds): *A Companion to Chrétien de Troyes* (Woodbridge, 2005)

Mabey, R.: *Flora Britannica: The Definitive New Guide to Wild Flowers, Plants and Trees* (London, 1996)

Mallett, M.: *Mercenaries and their Masters: Warfare in Renaissance Italy* (London, 1974)

Malory, Sir Thomas: *Le Morte D'Arthur in Two Volumes* (ed. J. Cowen) (Harmondsworth, 1969)

McKisack, M.: *The Fourteenth Century, 1307–1399* (Oxford, 1959)

Monmouth, Geoffrey of: *The History of the Kings of Britain* (trans. L. Thorpe) (Harmondsworth, 1966)

Ohlgren, T. H. (ed.): *Medieval Outlaws: Ten Tales in Modern English* (Stroud, 1998)

Offord, M. Y. (ed.): *The Parlement of the Thre Ages* (Oxford, 1959)

Oman, C. W. C.: *A History of the Art of War in the Middle Ages: Vol. II: 1278–1485* (London, 1898)

Prestwich, M.: *Armies and Warfare in the Middle Ages: The English Experience* (New Haven and London, 1996)

Pritchard, V.: *English Medieval Graffiti* (Cambridge, 1967)

Saul, N.: *Richard II* (New Haven and London, 1997)

Sayers, D. L.: *The Song of Roland* (Harmondsworth, 1957)

Sisam, K. (ed.): *Fourteenth Century Verse & Prose* (Oxford, 1921)

Smith, M. T. A.: *Sir Gawain and the Green Knight: A New Telling of the Fourteenth Century Alliterative Masterpiece* (London, 2018)

Strickland, M. and Hardy, R.: *The Great Warbow: From Hastings to the Mary Rose* (Stroud, 2005)

Sumption, J.: *The Hundred Years War, Vol. 1: Trial by Battle* (London, 1990)

Sumption, J.: *The Hundred Years War, Vol. 2: Trial by Fire* (London, 1999)

Sumption, J.: *The Hundred Years War, Vol. 3: Divided Houses* (London, 2009)

Trigg, S. (ed.): *Wynnere and Wastoure* (Oxford, 1990)

Turville-Petre, T.: *The Alliterative Revival* (Cambridge, 1977)

ACKNOWLEDGEMENTS

I am indebted once more to my wife, Nicky Parker, who has tolerated King Arthur taking over practically all our spare time since I began work on the book eighteen months ago. As with *Sir Gawain and the Green Knight*, I thank Nick Wray, who has provided exceptional motivational support throughout the writing process. Sue Jones of Stoneman Press in the county of Essex is also due a special mention: all the illustrations in this book have been produced on her presses and, throughout, her encouragement, advice and guidance have been of huge support. Sue is an exceptional tutor, talent and friend. In this way, I am also grateful to Anna Pye and Tracey Ashman, fellow members of a small printmaking group we founded several years ago, who have always offered great support (not forgetting biscuits and, in Tracey's case, some particularly good cake). Not insignificantly, I'd also like to acknowledge Richard O'Connor with whom, as a boy, I fought out countless knight battles on the dining room table with Timpo model soldiers and Britains' *Swoppet* knights; the bloodshed and anatomical utterances during which have now come back to haunt me with this book – there is a strange similarity between those battles and the ones described in the *Alliterative Morte Arthure*! Mike Ashman. Stuart Handysides and Alex Young have also been helpful in working through some of the poem's metrical elements during a production of an abridged version of this translation at St James Church, Stanstead Abbotts in November 2019. Andrew Barnwell, Sarah Parker, Paul Joyce, Jane Everard, Anne Sauntson and Nick and Julie Scarr must also gain a mention: having enthusiastic friends who always see the positive is such a blessing, especially in those moments of lonely self-doubt in the darker writing days. In the same way, every supporter who has pledged money to make this happen, many of whom I do not know but who are all named in the back, must be thanked: it could not have happened without you. At Unbound, Simon Spanton, the editor who initially signed me up for this work, Georgia Odd and Imogen Denny are all due a special mention, as are the rest of the editorial and production team. I particularly thank Lindeth Vasey who has brought exceptional rigour to bear on this book. Finally, I am conscious that during the last year, this book has taken up so much of my time that I have neglected many of my friends who frankly deserve better. I hope they can forgive me my silence at times; in this small way, I would like to acknowledge each and every one of them for their unspoken support and for their understanding

.

A NOTE ON THE AUTHOR

Michael Smith is from Cheshire. He studied history at the University of York and printmaking at the Curwen Print Study Centre near Cambridge. He has a particular interest in the Alliterative Revival of the fourteenth century; his first book, an illustrated translation of *Sir Gawain and the Green Knight*, was published by Unbound in 2018.

www.mythicalbritain.co.uk